WILD MOON HEALING REVOLUTION

Expand Your Energy Healing Network to Empower the Warrior Within

Go beyond Wild Moon Healing and connect to the healing powers of a vast energetic network and holistic therapies to invoke different energies that support spiritual, mental, emotional, and physical growth and transformation.

by
Donna S. Conley

ISBN Paperback: # 979-8-9863114-4-9
ISBN Hardcover: # 979-8-9863114-6-3
ISBN Electronic: # 979-8-9863114-5-6

Library of Congress Control Number: 9798986311449

Book cover artwork by: Lara Conley

Publisher: Wild Moon Healers LLC / Donna Conley

1296 Cronson Blvd., # 3128
Crofton, MD 21114-9998
www.wildmoonhealers.com

Printed in the United States of America.

Disclaimer:

No material in this book is intended to be a substitute for professional health advice, diagnosis, or treatment. Always seek the advice of your physician or other qualified healthcare provider with any questions you may have regarding a medical or mental health condition or treatment and before undertaking a new health-care regimen, and never disregard professional medical advice or delay in seeking it because of anything you have read in this book.

WILD
MOON
HEALING
REVOLUTION

*I dedicate this book to all the Wild Moon Healers out there.
Stay authentic.*

CONTENTS

WILD MOON HEALING REVOLUTION

ACKNOWLEDGEMENTS

First, a humble thank you to someone I've never met. Jaclyn Barnes, I appreciate you and the comments on the two-star Amazon rating you left for my book *Wild Moon Healing*. You wanted more information about the moon, and my first thought was, "Well, it's so much more than just the moon." And then I just couldn't stop writing. I hope this book finds you on your journey and you appreciate it, because you did, in a sense, help to inspire it.

To my sister, Lara, thank you for letting me be your sidekick! I may throw you under the bus sometimes with my stories, but that is because we have the best stories! It's never a dull moment when the two of us are together. I love you, sis. Let's keep manifesting.

To my editorial team, Christina Griffin and Zora Knauf. Christina, my talented niece, I appreciate your level of effort in editing my book and helping me achieve a well-written manuscript. I appreciate and love you very much. Zora, I appreciate your professionalism and thank you for all your hard work. Your thoroughness and attention to detail is much welcomed. I highly recommend your services.

Kristen Wise and Maira Pedreira, thank you for your professionalism and stellar work ethic. I have complete faith and trust in your abilities, which is why I chose to work with you again. From the bottom of my heart, thank you.

HELLO!

Hi, I'm Donna, owner of Wild Moon Healers. I help people transform and create a life they love.

As an advocate for mental health, a moon healer, energy coach, and national bestselling author, I help people raise their energetic vibration. I teach harnessing the energy of lunar cycles as a foundation to help you create a daily practice that works for you on your spiritual and healing path and to support you in creating your best life.

In my coaching practice I use somatic healing modalities such as meditation, sound healing, breathwork, Reiki, and energy healing to help you restore your true self, heal from the effects of trauma, and make behavioral changes. There are so many amazing energy and healing modalities available, but you need to create a routine or practice that is meaningful to you and that you are confident you will follow every month, all month long. I can help you discover your ability to change and craft a life you love. My process provides you with a starting place when you don't know where to begin and creates a structured approach to living authentically, one moon at a time.

Please take advantage of this energy healing knowledge to strengthen your spirituality and heal the trauma that's trapped in your body, among many other benefits. This is an excellent opportunity to involve your heart, mind, and body in the healing process. I hope that this book will provide you with a variety of energetic influences and healing modalities to consider to help you enhance or create a daily practice that works best for you. Through this book I challenge you to forget what you think you know and discover what is true for you. This manuscript provides a description of the energetic network we all have access to, illustrates how everything is connected, cyclical, and balanced, and teaches you how to harness these energies. To help you enhance your Moon work and how you follow lunar cycles, this book embarks on an exploration of the many types of energy available to you, including much more than moon energy. If you work with lunar energy, you are working with nature and all that implies.

The basic premise of this book is that if you sync with nature and energies from above, including the moon, your life will fall into a natural rhythm. This provides you with grace when you need it and encourages you to give it all you've got. Stop burning the candle at both ends, going after a goal when the energy doesn't support it, and feeling as though you let yourself or others down when things don't work out. You want to give people the best of you, not what's left of you. Get in sync with nature and allow your life to unfold naturally while you work to create change that supports the experience you want to live and the person you want to be. The energetic network surrounds you all the time, and you can tap into it at any moment. Know that everything shows up vibrationally before it appears experientially. To have a positive life you must raise your energetic frequency to attract higher-vibing experiences. This book helps you connect to the vast energetic network available to everyone and regulate your own energy, thereby raising your vibration.

Stay Authentic!

1

ENERGETIC NETWORK

What Is the Energetic Network?

If you've read my book *Wild Moon Healing*, then you know I teach following lunar cycles to create your best life. That book outlined a structured approach to following lunar cycles that shifts focus as the phases of the moon change. However, lunar energy is only a small part of the overall energetic network used in energy healing. There exists a vast interconnected network that allows for movement, or energetic flow; these different and varied energy components communicate with one another for this purpose. The inner workings of this energetic network are much grander and more intricate than anyone can fathom but include your own personal energy, Gaia (Mother Earth), and Source (God/a higher power/universe/angels), as well as the moon.

In writing this book, I do not assume that the idea of energy and its influence, healing ability, and universal connection is familiar to you. This book draws from my experience and research. I encourage you, however, to keep an open mind. Concepts you may reject at first might become understandable and even credible as you study ideas and practices that grasp your attention and curiosity.

Metaphysical wisdom dates back to ancient cultures. The teachings of these ancient cultures are still relevant and valuable today, despite our temporal distance. Metaphysics is the branch of philosophy that studies the fundamental nature of reality. This includes topics such as existence, time, and identity. Defining reality and knowledge is theoretical and abstract, but many of the well-known ancient Greek philosophers such as Plato, Socrates, Aristotle, and Heraclitus were doing just that thousands of years ago, and their contributions to the field of philosophy are still highly valued today.

The most relevant question to ask when relating ancient wisdom to Wild Moon Healing is, "How do I get to know myself?" That is the ultimate question. Proven healing modalities can help you answer this question at an innate physical level. Part of the process is to unlearn what you think you know and accept that you don't know what you don't know. Some of the concepts in this book require faith to receive guidance from above as well as ancestral wisdom. I urge you to read with an open mind—to suspend your disbelief—but also question my guidance. Forget what you think you know to discover your truth and your authentic self who remembers and begins to have glimpses of higher energetic influences, beings, and experiences. This concept is called *being present* or simply being. You cannot correspond within this energetic network, to celestial bodies, or tangible energy from Earth at any moment other than now.

The Hermetic principle of correspondence, "As above, so below,"[1] is a powerful statement that expresses this energy connection. In Wild Moon Healing language, we use this

---

[1] Hermes Trismegistus, The Emerald Tablet of Hermes.

same principle, "as within, so without," to refer to how our internal communication results in self-care and relationships with other energies, such as earth. Your divine energy, or inner magic, is reflected to the outside world through this internal energetic interaction. How you outwardly care for yourself determines your level of inner self-esteem and the vibration at which your energy resonates, which is the root of all your experiences. The energetic influence of how you interpret your experience creates your self-talk and daily habits (as within), and the level of vibration you internalize from the experience radiates outward for the rest of the world to see (so without). This concept speaks of balance, which you will notice is one of the major themes of this book.

Of course, this view describes someone living authentically, which is how you maintain your personal equilibrium. We are all masters of self-deceit. We all have false beliefs and tend to hold them close due to our negative life events that we don't want to reexperience. All of the events in your life create feelings, thoughts, and actions and send a frequency through the energetic network. This happens all the time, whether you live truthfully or insincerely. Accepting how your thoughts and actions interact with everything outside of you can spark a desire to break negative behavioral and thought patterns, or, in this case, initiate the Wild Moon Healing process. I suggest that rather than continuing to create new habits, which is something all of us try to do time and time again, you can use your personal energy to heal from the effects of your trauma and create new daily practices. Energy is always here to help you establish a new spiritual routine, lose weight, or tackle whatever it is you are presently working on in your life.

Healing yourself energetically not only helps you but also the rest of the world. As others experience high-vibrational energy from you, you help to heal them. Your positive energy can affect them greatly in their time of need. This is because all that you do creates an energetic footprint, the beginning of an energetic ripple effect, where your energy moves through time and space to affect generations yet to come. This energy can even move backwards through time to touch and even heal your ancestral lineage. The opposite is true as well. If your energy is vibrating at low levels, that is what you are presenting to the world, and it will become your legacy.

Leaving behind a positive energetic influence can only be accomplished when you are living in alignment with your authentic self and in the present moment. Find your true self through energy healing and connecting to and working with all energetic sources available to you. In this book, I discuss many types of celestial, tangible, and internal energy sources that you can harness to create your best life. Tap into these energies to heal your own energy. As you heal, you will begin to curate the life you want, one that you absolutely love and can be proud of. Gaze at the following image that portrays this energetic network and see what this means to you. Take note in a journal of what comes up for you before you read any further, because what you believe matters.

As Above – Source

There are many applications and specific interpretations of the phrase "as above," but I use the phrase to represent an energetic connection with your Source and divine guides. This book will not debate or provide you the answer to whether or not there is a God. That is something you must figure out on your own. In order to do so, I urge you to reject your beliefs that came from your upbringing (religion and cultural) and human experience (false limiting beliefs) up to this point in your life. My desire is for you to be whom you were born to be—the person you were before the world told you who you should be—and the person your soul intended for you to be. If, after practicing Moon work and working with energy, you arrive at the same response to the question at hand as your younger self would have, then great! Fundamentally, I'm saying that you should know what you believe and why you believe it, but with passion rather than mechanically. Having family, culture, or society dictate to you what your truth is versus discovering it for yourself are vastly different experiences. Growing up in a religious household and mechanically going through the motions lacks meaning and depth of feeling; this is completely different from experiential learning on a spiritual level—truly experiencing God's love, nature's bounty, higher-self connection, or angelic support.

You need faith, which is your connection to your support team, to unlearn your false belief system of self. This can be difficult because in all likelihood, some sort of traumatic or negative experience internally shaped the things you believe about yourself. This is the case for most of us. Your subconscious could be running false beliefs such as "I am not important" or "I am unworthy of love." You need to decide what's true for you and who you are authentically. Because you are reading this book, that in and of itself suggests you do believe in something greater than yourself, and in other dimensions of being. How else could this vast energetic network be available to us, and how else could you connect to it?

There are no wrong answers to faith. Whether you believe there is a difference between Source and God or you believe they are one and the same is entirely personal to your interpretations and your beliefs. It doesn't matter what you call your Source, the words you use to define it, or how you see it in your mind's eye. What you believe is your truth; it doesn't need to be argued or defined.

Most people believe human existence is about defining, labeling, putting things in a nice, neat little box—these things make people feel safe and provide them with a sense of knowing. While I personally hate these metaphorical boxes, as they make me feel imprisoned, I respect anyone who believes differently than me. If I didn't, my consciousness would not have expanded to the point of writing books about energy. Through my personal connection with God, energy, and spirit guides, I've discovered my passion for helping others. It's funny that I have been helping people all along in my professional life, but now I am doing so much more purposefully and with passion. I want to use my connection to this energetic network to encourage myself to talk about struggles, trauma, and depression in order to help initiate healing conversations with others so we can get ourselves out of the metaphorical boxes in which we find ourselves.

People have always and still try to put me in a metaphorical box, but I choose liberation. You cannot experience true freedom from within the confines of the definitions set by others. Don't disappear into a culture of following paths well established by others. You can evolve back into the mystery and wonder of your own life. Since I began Wild Moon Healers, family and friends have questioned my beliefs and told me that I am creating my own religion. Teaching myself and inquiring about things consciously unknown to me before is not me reinventing the wheel; rather, it is the path to personal growth and transformation. My journey may look vastly different than yours, as it should, because without diversity there wouldn't be much to talk about or explore. There are more people like me out there than some people may think... people who grew up going to church and have since evolved into this expansive consciousness and spirituality, while holding onto their faith. Spiritual Christians don't complain, even when under persecution. If you want to put me in a box, I will choose the term *Witchy Baptist* because of my connection to the earth. Christianity is not something that a person is but is something a person *does*. Nothing about the Wild Moon Healing process means leaving your beliefs behind; rather, the idea of what you believe has shifted and grown. At least that is my experience. If your experience seems similar to mine, or the exact opposite for that matter, engage me in conversation through email at dsconley@wildmoonhealers.com or through social media @WildMoonHealers. I would love to hear your story; you matter.

Regardless of your beliefs, the topic of "as above" is magnanimous and includes God, angels, guides, ascended masters, higher self, and your ancestral energy, which are all available to you. You can connect to them at any time to help you manifest practically anything into your life. Jesus himself was a nomad with no worldly possessions, yet he manifested fish from empty seas, wine from water, and the entire last supper... His needs were always met. He was the ultimate manifestor, and you can be too.

Personal Energy Centers

You can connect with the energetic network through your personal energy system, which is made up of meridian pathways and chakras. Energy is the foundation of all matter, and it is always flowing and changing. The physical body has veins and arteries to help support life via a beating heart, and it has nerves and organs to support our bodily functions, but it also has an intelligent energy system. The nervous system transmits a variety of cognitive, emotional, and experiential elements energetically through the body. The subtle energetic body is comprised of energetic pathways known as meridians that flow with prana (or life force energy) and converge at powerful energy centers in the body known as chakras. How you treat yourself and others is a reflection of how your energy is flowing throughout your energy centers. Your chakras can be wide open: where you may find yourself in fits of rage; balanced: where you are in good mental and physical health; closed: where you may find yourself experiencing depressive episodes; or anything in between. Ultimately, the chakra system is an energetic infrastructure that supports your mental, emotional, and spiritual well-being. You can use other energetic sources to establish a healing plan to help shift and move your own energy through the chakra system.

While there are many chakras in the body, the body's energy system has seven main chakras situated along the spine, beginning at the base of your spine, and extending through the crown of your head. You can revitalize your internal energetic network by focusing on each chakra to release stagnant energy, align your energetic body, raise your vibration, and free your authentic self. Envision your body as a cup, with energy flowing in your head from your Source and also up through your feet, as if an electrical cord were plugged into the earth. The importance of these connections is that they feed your energetic body and raise the vibrational frequency of your energy. You can lose energy through energetic leaks. There are so many different kinds of energetic leaks, but some common ones include not sleeping well, hating your job, being in a negative relationship, or being around energetic vampires. There are many ways to protect your personal energy, but the first step is having awareness that it exists.

The first of the main chakras is the root chakra. This energy center is red in color and circles the base of your spine. Its energetic quality helps you feel grounded and safe and serves to keep you connected. When you are stable, you are more able to connect with the truth of who you are. Through the root chakra you create balance with that which is below and above.

The second chakra—the sacral chakra—has a lively energy. It's an orange-colored energy circling at your pelvic floor and lower abdomen. This chakra connects you with your creativity and sexuality; this helps you find pleasure in the truth of who you are by reaching your creative potential.

The third chakra is your solar plexus. A yellow-colored energy circling the powerhouse in your belly helps you realize your self-confidence and connects to your inner spark, enabling you to act on your truth.

The heart chakra is your fourth energy center. It's a green-colored energy circling at the center of your chest. When balanced, the heart chakra expresses love, compassion, and forgiveness, which, in turn, helps you to learn to love the truth of who you are.

The fifth charka is the throat chakra. It's a blue-colored energy circling at the center of your throat and helps you express yourself through communication and listening. This energy helps you speak the truth of who you are and what deeply moves you with conviction.

The sixth chakra is your third eye. It's an indigo-colored energy circling between your eyebrows that opens your conscious mind to your inner wisdom and helps you translate what you see so that you can interpret what it means to you.

The last major chakra in your personal energy network is the crown chakra. It's a violet-colored energy circling just above the top of your head, through which you can experience divine enlightenment and connect with your divine truth.

ENERGY

I am connected	ॐ	I understand my truth
I admire my responses	ॐ	I see my truth
I know myself	हं	I speak my truth
I love myself	यं	I love my truth
I trust myself	रं	I act on my truth
I am free	वं	I create my truth
I feel safe within	लं	I am grounded in my truth

FLOWS WITHIN

For the purpose of this book, understand that the duality of the chakra system creates balance within. The bottom three chakras (root, sacral, and solar plexus) represent how your energy relates to or works with the energy in your external environment and connects to tangible things such as the earth. When you are authentic and strongly rooted in your truth, your outside world reflects it. You live an uninhibited life when outside sources don't affect your freedom to adapt to your situation in a way that makes you feel comfortable. When you trust your intuition to guide you without any doubt, you can power through anything. Your heart center urges you to surrender and accept things that are out of your control for your peace of mind. The chakras work together, so if you can't anchor your truth or don't feel safe, you certainly will not feel free or trust your intuition. This disharmony can have immense power over your physical and mental well-being. You may manifest a physical health issue, or worse, you may develop addictions that will have long-term effects on your health. However, when in balance, you manage life's situations with the ability to let go of what no longer serves you, breaking the chains created by past experiences, and you can live free. As you manifest the life you want, you are calling in an energy that takes tangible form. This requires you to be strongly rooted to the earth. Trying to shift your energy from an ungrounded place only leads to temporary manifestations because you have no foundation to build upon.

The top three chakras (throat, third eye, and crown) relate to your spiritual energy and connection to your Source and other celestial beings as well as your integrity, expression, intuition, and awakening. Living authentically includes speaking your truth, interpreting the truth of what you see and how it relates to you, and understanding your life's purpose. When your crown chakra is open and balanced, you feel intimately connected to your Source, God, or creator energy. We are spiritual beings having a human experience; therefore, your inner spark will always long for a way back to Source or connection to all that is above. Your heart center, the fourth chakra, is a bridge that connects your spiritual energy with incarnate energy. This chakra is the center of your body's energetic system. It sits over your physical heart for a reason. It acts like your physical heart, only it doesn't help with blood flow; it promotes energetic flow. From this place you can not only help yourself but the entire planet. Your energy can promote love and compassion and travel across time and space. When you balance your chakra system, your soul is content because its need for love, community, creativity, connection with the divine, and authenticity is satisfied.[2] The energy from your chakras radiates from your heart center and leaves your energetic footprint everywhere you go.

---

[2] Parita Shah, "What the Chakras Teach Us About the Mind and Body Connection," https://chopra.com/articles/what-the-chakras-teach-us-about-the-mind-and-body-connection.

Tangible things have energetic footprints as well. For example, your root chakra governs the old energy of money, which is also where feelings of lack and fear originate. Once upon a time, money was only material, and real things you can touch. As such, people bartered a chicken for a sack of seeds, shook hands to solidify a deal, and wrote checks to pay bills, which they then mailed through the postal system. The new energy of money is heart centered, and thus comes from your heart chakra. People now spend money based on feelings and personal beliefs. Some use money to support sustainably sourced items and hold business owners to high social standards, such as inclusiveness and fair labor practices. Now people transmit money electronically; direct debits occur digitally, and many of us use payment apps for spending and bill payments.

Living with the false limiting belief that there is never enough money stems from old generational energy patterns encoded into your root chakra, creating the energy of lack (i.e., an issue with your safety). This extends to lack of abundance, worthiness, or significance in this life. Expressing gratitude for all that you have creates the energy of abundance and is heart centered. The truth about money is that it is neither good nor bad; it's just another form of energy used in energetic transactions intensified by your personal energy and beliefs. What you spend your money on is a reflection of your inner self and the flow of your energy.

Inside your body, the bottom energy centers work together with your upper energy centers. If you are rooted in your truth and really connected (root chakra), you will have an easier time speaking your truth (throat chakra). This includes feeling safe and expressing healthy boundaries that maintain your safety and peace of mind. When you are genuinely happy with who you are (sacral chakra), you intuitively interpret your environment and gain useful insights about your situation (third-eye chakra). Experiencing divine enlightenment and genuinely knowing your truth (crown chakra) prepares you to act on your truth, igniting the powerhouse in your belly (solar plexus chakra). All of this energy transmutes through your heart center (heart chakra), allowing you to express love, compassion, and absolution when vibrating at a high frequency. When you convey a low-vibrational energetic expression of anger, such as road rage, then you are in need of energetic healing, which will ultimately help your energy centers to cycle at a higher frequency.

Chakra is a Sanskrit word that means wheel or cycle. As you will discover in this book, all energy goes through cycles. But more specifically for your energy centers, they spin to help with your personal energetic flow through meridian pathways in your body and work with your nervous system. These pathways allow energy to flow, like water flowing in a stream, into the chakras. The energy in the chakras moves in a circular motion, and its speed affects the vibration of your energy. Consider the way a wind turbine uses air that flows in various patterns and speeds to create energy/electricity. Your energy flows in various patterns, and its speed reflects either heavy, slow-moving energy caused by energetic leaks and false and limiting beliefs or light, faster-moving energy caused by preventive or restorative care. Like attracts like, so the more care you practice through Wild Moon Healing principles, the faster your energy will move, thus increasing the vibration you send out into the universe. A high-vibrational energy becomes magnetic, attracting higher energetic experiences and resources into your life.

How do you know if your energy is open or closed, or moving too fast or too slow? The answer lies in your emotions, physically expressed by mood, how much your environment influences your actions, how you outwardly treat yourself and others, and the state of your physical health. All emotions, including ones such as anger, are valid and teach you valuable things about yourself. A high-vibrational expression of anger would result in something upsetting you, so you either form a healthy boundary so it can't upset you in that way again, or your passion ignites, causing you to speak out about an injustice in the world. It may even cause you to change your vocation so your daily work reflects this. Feelings such as sadness or depression slow down your energetic flow and send a message to you through your nervous system that something is not right. When you connect to your energy, you receive the messages in a timely manner so you can make changes in your life—which will prevent those low-vibing emotions from creating significant issues. In the same way, hyperactivity, insomnia, or impulse control is an energetic message that your energy centers are wide open and spinning too fast.

One easy way to change the energetic flow of your chakra system is through music. Albert Einstein once said, "Everything in our universe is a vibration." Energy creates vibrations or sound when transferred through the correct medium. There are musical notes, sounds, and instruments that correspond with each chakra to help balance them. This is why attending a soundbath or listening to instrumental music is so relaxing—it's balancing you.

Sound and Chakras

- Root – Resonates with the element of earth, all earth zodiac signs, and the shape of a square or cube. The musical note C, the mantra of LAM, and the drums are associated with this chakra.
- Sacral – Resonates with the element of water and all water zodiac signs as well as the shape of a circle. The musical note D, the mantra of VAM, and strings are associated with this chakra.
- Solar Plexus – Resonates with the element of fire and all fire zodiac signs, as well as the shape of a triangle. The musical note E, the mantra of RAM, and horn are associated with this chakra.

- Heart – Resonates with the heart and a higher expression of all zodiac signs, as well as the shape of a cross. The musical note F, the mantra of YAM, and flute or wind instruments are associated with this chakra.
- Throat – Resonates with the element of air and all the air zodiac signs, as well as the shape of a chalice (a cup). The musical note G, the mantra of HAM, and instead of an instrument, the voice is fittingly associated with this chakra.
- Third Eye – Resonates with thought and is a higher expression of all signs, as well as the shape of the start of David. The musical note A and the mantra of OM are associated with this chakra.
- Crown – Resonates with light and is a higher expression of all signs, as well as the shape of a lotus. The musical note B and silence are associated with this chakra.

Solfeggio frequencies are a set of nine electromagnetic tones that are reputed to have the power to heal and raise consciousness. If you ever had a music class in school, then Do, Re, Mi, Fa, Sol, La, Ti, Do may sound familiar. Those sounds came from the scale—C, D, E, F, G, A, B, C—and we just read how those notes match each chakra. Listening to crystal singing bowls is relaxing because of the vibration they create; however, solfeggio tones, also related to chakras, are different because they are also healing on a cellular level. They help to open up energy centers, move stagnant energy, and heal by vibrationally clearing some of the effects of traumatic or negative experiences. I use solfeggio tuning forks in my practice for this reason; they assist in managing personal energy. The key to managing your energy is to find your balance. You can find balance in simple things your doctor may have told you about many times, such as diet and exercise, but as you now know, that is such a small piece to the puzzle. When you tap into the universal flow of energy, you have constant access to a never-ending source of energy to help you create abundance and ignite creativity. In the same way you use your personal energy system to connect with your Source, you can also use it to connect with the energy that the Earth provides.

So Below – Earth

Gaia is the primal mother goddess, complete in herself, and ancestral mother of all life. I will discuss modes later, of which earth is an element (rather than an energetic goddess source). The land we live on would not exist without the other elements. Elements work together, as your personal energy system does, to create the ecosystem that you live in, which establishes the message that we need the Earth more than it needs us— the Earth exists for us. Gaia was the first goddess in Greek mythology who brought forth the heavens, because it created a safety net on all sides for her. She knew the importance of balance and the need for love and connection since she was born of Chaos—the beginning of all things. The Greeks swore an oath to the primordial goddess, believing her strength is why no one could escape the Earth in human form. In modern times and in a scientific sense, the term "Gaia" means the complete living planet itself, as a complex organism.[3] Activities such as earthing and just being in nature are well-known, popular ways to reenergize your chakras and raise your vibration. Too bad those engaging in nature spirituality don't always respect her, thus the improper disposal of their trash. You are an extension of the Earth and the cosmos, so you should respect and honor them in the same way you should love and honor yourself.

---

[3] de Traci Regula, "Gaia: The Greek Goddess of the Earth," June 26, 2019, https://www.thoughtco.com/greek-mythology-gaia-1525978.

They say love makes the world go 'round, but I believe it's more specific than that: Through the act of loving yourself, you create and grow more love to give from within yourself. Therefore, self-love is what makes the world go 'round.

The earth connects through your feet to your root chakra, making you feel safe, grounded, and supported. Carol Tuttle said, "Before you can take your first step to awakening, you have to choose to stand." As soon as you make the decision to stand for your truth or authenticity, the universe jumps into action and supports you. Connecting to the earth's energy is equally as important as connecting with all of the universe's energy, including your Source, your guides, angels, and loving ancestors. Become aware of your connection with the earth and how you move through the day, because there is a correlation.

Do you feel supported, strong, or confident in all that you do? Being mindful is an empowering tool and an important part of spiritual wellness. To help you connect to Gaia, view the Earth as a living being that helps you thrive with an open heart and live in the flow of abundance. Acknowledge how living with compassion for Earth and all living things is the foundation for a healthy spiritual practice. Many of the nature-based practices surging now, including astrology, crystals, and shamanism, are thousands of years old because she's always been with us, only people seemed to have forgotten that as time has passed over the centuries.

Finding spiritual healing through nature can awaken the energetic healing power that already exists within you. Connecting with energy is a two-way street. Not only can the Earth add a sense of vigor to your personal energy, but she also accepts your energy (good or bad) and can compost it, turning it into more of nature's bounty. If you are new on your spiritual and/or healing path, reconnecting with the Earth and nature is the easiest way to begin because it is accessible to everyone.

Moon Phases

With all this talk about energy and Moon work, you should learn about the different phases of the moon and how to use its energy. Use the moon to remind you when it's time to set intentions, assess a goal, or conduct shadow work. There is tremendous power in harnessing the energy and rhythm of the moon and its phases. The moon plays a huge role in balancing your life physically, emotionally, mentally, and spiritually. It also influences manifestation and attraction of the things that will help you live your best life. It is as if the phases of the moon exist to create an intelligent, straightforward road map for manifesting. Tuning into the phases of the moon provides you with a structured approach to help you take consistent action toward achieving your goals.

The moon represents powerful divine feminine energy, giving life to matters of new beginnings, transformation, renewal, and release to help you create balance in your life. Once attuned to the moon's energy and its cycles, you activate her innate powers and embody her natural qualities of grace, creativity, femininity, transformation, and change. A new moon is like a blank slate that can help you discover what you want. The energy from a waxing moon is powerful in directing you into action and also helps you explore how you are triggered or react to people, places, and things. The energy of a full moon helps you explore your shadows. Most people believe a full moon has negative energy because of the way people behave when the moon is full, but the truth is its job is to balance energy. You will gain a better understanding of this as you continue to read. The energy during the waning moon signifies a time for gratitude, forgiveness, and surrender. It is a counterpart creating balance with the waxing moon phase. Under a waxing moon, you refine your outward, forward-moving actions (masculine energy), and during the waning moon phase, it's time to reflect on how you feel and show yourself grace (feminine energy).

Moon Phases

New	Waxing	First	Waxing	Full	Waning	Last	Waning	New
Moon	Crescent	Quarter	Gibbous	Moon	Gibbous	Quarter	Crescent	Moon

Remember, energy connects everything, and everything you say, think, and do can provide insight into how to change your life. My first book, *Wild Moon Healing*, provides in-depth information on lunar cycles with specific activities that change perspective as the moon transitions through all its phases. By synchronizing your activities to specific phases of the moon and working with the energy it presents, you can amplify the effect of your Moon work.

Wild Moon Healing

Wild Moon Healing is a program that follows lunar cycles, and thus uses energy and nature to guide your life and spiritual practice. This process helps you connect to your energy source of that which is above, below, and within your personal energy system. Admiring the beauty of the moon helps cultivate a relationship with nature, while its mystery helps cultivate a relationship with the unknown and unseen. Through Wild Moon Healing, you laterally go after your goals, learn from your life experiences, heal, and transform your life by harnessing the energy of all that is. To manifest with the moon, you must become aware of lunar and astrological energy but also connect to the collective energetic network that follows nature all year long. When connected, you can feel normal monthly energy around new and full moons up to a couple of days before and after they occur. Comparably, in a collective sense, equinox and solstice energy can last a couple of weeks, much like the amplified energy during eclipse season. Since the moon's energy causes the Earth's orbit to vary slightly, the regularity of the orbit is officially defined by the Sun. This makes sense when you examine the feminine energy of a lunar cycle versus the masculine energy of the Sun. Since all is connected, I relate lunar cycles and Moon work to a global scale based on the seasons.

The energy of lunar cycles represented by the calendar year energetically affects the collective. Slightly tilted on its axis, the Earth travels around the Sun, providing various amounts of sunlight to different points on Earth at contrasting times of the year, providing us with the change of seasons. There are two equinoxes and two solstices per year that usher in the energy of change. Equinox energy is strong—just as the energy from a new

CALENDAR YEAR	vs	LUNAR CYCLES
Spring Equinox / Lunar New Year		New Moon
Summer Solstice		Frist Quarter Moon
Fall Equinox		Full Moon
Winter Solstice		Last Quarter Moon

See how the calendar is one big lunar cycle?

WILDMOONHEALERS.COM

and full moon and occur in the spring and fall. The equinoxes occur every March (19, 20, or 21) and September (22 or 23). The day the equinox occurs is when the Sun is precisely above the equator, creating an equal proportion of daylight and darkness. Solstice energy matches that of a quarter moon during the waxing and waning phases, which is a significant part of the cycle occurring in summer and winter. A solstice occurs every June (20 or 21) and December (21 or 22). A solstice happens when the Sun is farthest from the equator, providing us with our longest and shortest days of the year. In the Northern Hemisphere, June is the summer solstice and is the longest day of the year, while December is the winter solstice and is the shortest day of the year. A cardinal zodiac sign that ushers in a new season, thus accompanying the energy of change, occurs during the time of year that an equinox or solstice occurs.

As the seasons transform nature, that's your cue to initiate change in your life and perspective on various levels. Following moon phases will help you adjust to the changing energy of the seasons. New moon energy is about new beginnings. This energy starts with the spring equinox with a big-picture or dream for your life, thereby creating a future self with which you can correspond. Every month on the new moon you're beginning the process of "What can I do this month to get me closer to my big-picture goal and future self?" Since you cannot change everything at once, focus on one thing at a time during each lunar cycle. You experience the energy of the waxing lunar cycle as the new moon grows into fruition just before the full moon. This energy helps you go after your goals but also helps you learn more about yourself. For example, you may reflect on and examine how you react to stress or hurdles. The mid-point of the waxing cycle is the first quarter moon, which occurs on the summer solstice, also known as midsummer, where you really want to take inspired action toward your goals. On a monthly basis you closely look at the details of your current experience, but on the solstice you examine how far you've come since the spring equinox and what you can do to better approach your overall goals, then make any necessary changes.

The fall equinox is bursting with full moon energy that implores you to look within and conduct shadow work. As your energy work increases, you start to notice parts of you that you've hidden. Some people may describe themselves as broken or lost, but that is not the case—you are you, a whole person with a lifetime of experiences. Who you are at your core (your soul) is still there. It's not hiding; rather, it's protected. Many people who experience trauma push it down in their body. The focus is getting through the hardest time of your life, and as you learn to live with your pain, you push your feelings down where they are stored in all of your tissue, tendons, and muscles. In other words, as you learn to survive, you are not learning to love your entire self.

Allowing pain to surface so you can release it can hurt badly— both mentally and physically. It can be extremely difficult to process depending on how many coping mechanisms you've adopted over the years. Coping mechanisms or addictions keep your pain hidden and keep the version of you that was hurt protected. Look into ways to release trauma such as breathwork or sound healing meditations to supplement your current healing plan. Trauma changes the way the nervous system, brain, and emotional energy respond to your environment. Those emotional and mental traumas not only make you feel less confident about yourself, but they also impose physical limitations on your life.

Shadow work is not easy because trauma is not the only thing that surfaces. Truths about *you* also surface, truths about things you've done, how those things made you feel about yourself, and, moreover, how you believe others feel about you. Associated feelings of guilt and shame can be paralyzing when they surface. This is why the days grow shorter in the fall time of the year, to allow you more down time to be introspective and care for yourself. Full moon energy isn't always chaotic; it can be peacefully reflective and meditative. Nature also shows us how easy and beautiful change can be, as seen by the landscape changing from green to vibrant reds, oranges, and yellows. The full moon energy associated with the seasonal change of fall is also your cue to create change in your life, but change is not always easy if you lack a sense of forgiveness and love for yourself.

Following the full moon energy of fall comes the waning lunar cycle and the winter solstice. The word *waning* means to fade away. We see this each month as the moon shrinks to a sliver then vanishes in the sky, and from a seasonal perspective, the amount of daylight is shorter. The global contemplative energy of this season makes personal transformation easier because increased darkness usually tends to decrease the amount of social activity you engage in. The work of surrendering is difficult and requires self-love, forgiveness of self, and physical rest. There is a pretense to surrender and let go that may require being truthful. As the proverbial saying goes, "Apologies unspoken keeps things broken." Really take time to contemplate the truths revealed to you by the full moon. Perhaps you must apologize to yourself for harmful ways you've treated your body, or the negative energy from a particular person may require a stronger boundary, or you must let that person go from your life entirely. As you transform, some people can't continue on your journey with you. Remember, the process is not about the other person, place, or thing in your life... It's about you and the influences your external environment has on you. You can also release negative energetic patterns that you've uncovered that your ego mind created from carrying around a false and limiting belief. This is why the theme of winter is to let go—surrender all that no longer serves you. This work is hard, so the short days and long nights are our cues from nature to rest more. You'll need it.

2

COSMIC INFLUENCES

The Astrological Year

While I correlate lunar energy to specific times of the year on a collective scale, the Sun drives the astrological year and, therefore, highly influences how you use lunar energy. Think about it. The moon reflects the Sun's light, and the Sun's energy helps the moon glow in the night sky. Therefore, it is also an integral part of the Wild Moon Healing process. The time the Sun takes to move through each zodiac sign is called a season. Each zodiac season lasts about four weeks, and regardless of your Sun sign, everyone can tap into the astrological energy of each zodiac sign.

The moon moves much faster and therefore transits the Earth in each astrological sign for a couple of days each month. Therefore, the zodiac influences much of the Moon work you will do. The attributes of each zodiac sign describe the astrological energy you will experience during each Sun season, as well as lunar transits. You have the entire zodiac in your birth chart—all twelve zodiac signs. For this reason, it is important to learn the traits of all the signs and the influence they can have on you, not just your Sun sign.

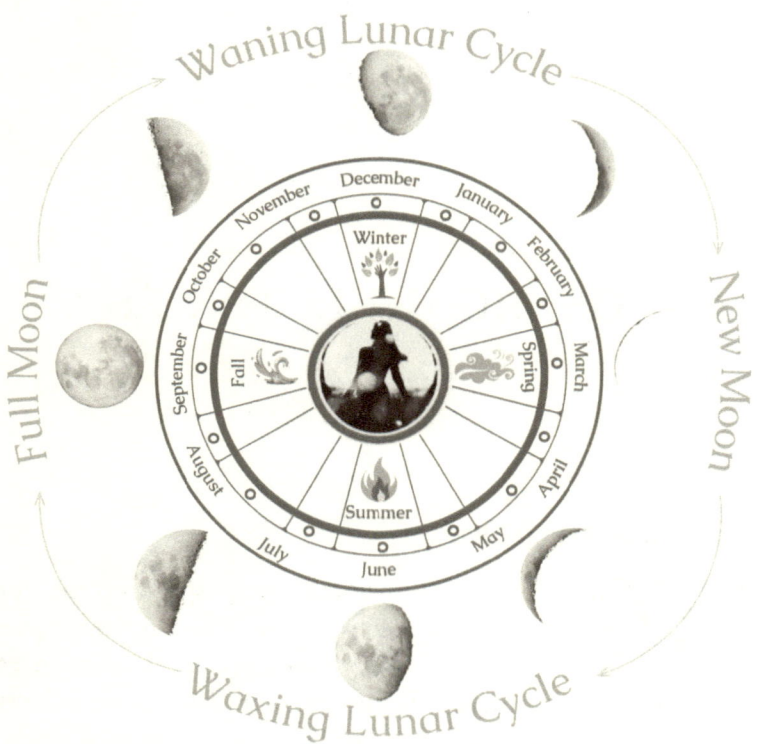

Spring Equinox

The spring equinox kicks off the astrological New Year as ruled by nature and the Sun sign of Aries. The collective energy matches that of the new moon. This is the time of year for any New Year's resolution, should you choose to make one! The motivational vibe of Aries ignites passion, positioning your energy, if you allow it, to become enthusiastic about conquering your biggest dream. Aries season, represented by ram energy, occurs from March 21 – April 19. This solar transition is always going to be a powerful time for setting intentions and refreshing your goals on big-picture items in your life, a task which you can start during the end of Pisces season—during the black moon energy. During Aries season, all signs of the zodiac can take advantage of the bold and spirited energy this time of year brings. Everyone can welcome the freshness of spring while summoning their inner warrior to welcome the opportunity of new beginnings and take initiative to embrace their authenticity.

The spring equinox energy continues through the Taurus and Gemini zodiac signs. Taurus season, represented by the bull, occurs from April 20 – May 20, and the collective moon energy starts to grow. This zodiac sign rules stability and security, helping you to not only focus in on your intention, goal, or big dream but also to start building on your foundation (i.e., the intentions you set) and also provides you with a sense that everything you want to create feels right. That is, it will feel right if you are going in the right direction. Trust what comes up for you. As far as healing, Taurus energy can raise your vibration, helping you to figure out who you want to be and where you are going in life. This time of year calls for pure honesty with self. If you stay in a place of self-deception, you are not honoring this energy or doing anything for your highest good. While it's okay to think and dream under this Sun sign, it is not a time for talking. Taurus season is about action, so start going after your dream—it's time to walk the walk.

Gemini season, represented astrologically by twins, makes May 21 – June 20 a busy time. The collective energy is that of a waxing crescent moon growing toward the first quarter moon. This time of year represents duality and finding balance and connection on the deepest of levels. You've started to act on your to-do list, which helps you gain momentum toward your dream, but since things don't always work out the way you plan, this double-sided energy can help you find middle ground. Tapping into this season's energy allows for clarifying murky situations and engaging your intellect with Gemini's talent for communication due to its ruling planet—Mercury. This planet loves its "F" words—such as fun, flirty, and frolicking. Gemini energy helps you perfect the wording of how you want your life to play out and with whom you may want to live your life with (i.e., refine that big dream if necessary). This time of year is an extremely social season after the long, dark months of winter, followed by two months of spring cleaning and finding your bearings. This energy can make your mind go in several directions at once. While being a social time, Gemini season is also about inner work and inspiring you to seek your truth. Doing Moon work during this time of year can help you grow as an individual and achieve personal milestones as you advance toward your goal. This balanced energy guides you from spring directly into the heat of summer.

Summer Solstice

The summer solstice is the collective energy equal to the first quarter moon energy of the waxing cycle and ushers in wise, nurturing, and emotive Cancer season. This zodiac is represented by the crab and occurs on June 21 – July 22. The Moon rules cancer, and its energies are strong this time of year, as seen in the way Cancer energy affects you on an emotional, mental, and creative level. This water sign doesn't exactly splash in excitement like the pool party you may attend during this time of year. Water signs are intuitive and perceptive. They are more sensitive than blunt and more magnetic than aggressive. This time of year may force you to delve into the deepest part of your emotions, but you don't have to do so alone. Make room for genuine care and allow the right people into your inner sanctum that can help you navigate this energy, if necessary. If you don't have a support network you trust, keep doing Moon work, and you will start to attract your tribe. The theme for the energy of summer solstice is about nurturing your closest bonds and sacred space. Based on the moon's influence under this sign and how it lines up with the energy of the first quarter moon, use emotions and instincts to direct your action. As you take meaningful action toward your goals, also begin to evaluate your progress. This energy helps you tap into your untampered logic to help you overcome obstacles and develop creative workarounds to any issues you have with your action plan, thus ensuring your success with what you are working on.

The summer solstice energy continues through Leo and Virgo. Leo season occurs from July 23 – August 22 and represents the collective moon energy just past the first quarter moon. It is a welcome respite after the heavy emotional energy of Cancer. Leo's energy is about creative expression, which can help you find alternative actions to any hurdles you are experiencing. The lion represents this bold, confident, and self-assured energy. It helps you to really exert energy on yourself and work toward your goals. Also, the energy of the lion puts an emphasis on the loyalty you have to yourself, allowing you to live by your true nature. The Sun rules Leo, and that planet oversees self-image, confidence, and identity. The fixed fire sign helps you stand strong in your power, passionately express yourself through creativity, and appreciate the bright side in any situation. Long days and increased vitamin-D exposure help you tackle your to-do list, expressing how much you care about yourself and what you are capable of achieving while soaking up the limelight! The nights are shorter during this time of year, coxing us to be active for longer periods of time. But, the star-studded night sky can really inspire your creative nature.

Virgo, represented by the maiden, occurs from August 23 – September 22. The collective moon energy is that of the waxing gibbous growing toward fruition. Thanks to the Sun's trip through your Sixth House, this season usually brings your focus to everyday tasks and your wellness routine. This mutable earth sign, ruled by Mercury, helps you to achieve balance and find magic in day-to-day things. Virgo's energy can help you reimagine and revamp your daily activities as a final effort to strive for your goals with all you've got before the collective full moon energy takes over in the fall. As it is an earth sign represented by the maiden, this energy can also ground you into a service-oriented mentality. It can be a hard switch from Leo energy, which was fun loving and extravagant, to the responsible energy of Virgo, but becoming organized, efficient, and overhauling your self-care regime will feel like a huge accomplishment! This energy is perfect for those with school-age children, teachers, and the like, helping you to organize daily life before the start of a new school year. It is also a wonderful time of year to do some "spring" cleaning to declutter and organize your living space as well as other areas of your life where you spend much of your time such as email and phone apps. Virgo's vibe celebrates the beauty of organization and the benefit of prioritizing your health and well-being, as well as caring for others.

Autumn Equinox

The autumn equinox occurs in the astrological sign of Libra and expresses full moon energy. Full moon energy can be potent and bring out the worst in people who do not engage in Moon work. However, by doing Moon work you will be able to access Libra energy to bring balance to your life with loving, social, and kind energy. This season, represented by the scales of justice and truth, occurs from

September 23 – October 22. Represented by the scales and the element of air, Libra energy ushers in a sense of fresh air and relief in the form of balance and beauty, making this an appropriate time to consider and invite balance into your life by exploring where you feel off. Venus, the planet of pleasure, rules Libra and embraces the energy of beauty and love. You need a lot of those qualities as the scales of justice turn inward, directing you to look at your shadows. During this time of year, you begin to spend more time in darkness and see the moon in the sky for longer periods of time. The fall equinox represents the end of the harvest season, so you can now reap the reward from all that hard work you've been doing since spring. It can be hard to balance a constantly shifting equilibrium of day-to-day life, so focus on your daily practices, morning routine, and nightly rituals to help transition your personal energy with the change of seasons. All the hustle and bustle of spring and summer may have depleted your energy stores. Nature knows this, so the days begin to wane, nudging you to move from a physical existence to one of intellectual energy—however, the spiritual pursuit of learning with this energy is introspective.

Autumn equinox energy continues through Scorpio and Sagittarius. Scorpio, represented by a scorpion, occurs from October 23 – November 21. The amazing colors of fall and the intense energy of this zodiac sign energetically suggest it is not satisfied with surface-level anything. Ruled by the action-oriented planet Mars, full of energy and sex, and the powerful transformational energy of Pluto, Scorpio energy is incredibly magnetic and intense—innately comfortable with the shadow side of life and sexuality. It exudes full moon energy on myriad levels. Full moon energy can be uncomfortable, as seen by the resolute and obstinate characteristic of Scorpios, so you may find it challenging to switch things up during this time of year. When you tap into this energy during the fall season, the universe supports your ability to form an emotional bond with someone you love, emerge vulnerable, build trust, and venture into intimidatingly uncharted waters through this emotionally charged, often spiritually satisfying time of year. But remember, the most important relationship is the one you have with yourself. If your current experience is unhealthy and negative, this time of year makes it easier to cultivate awareness and create a stronghold around any addiction or relationship that no longer serves you. Focus your energy on intimacy and personal transformation to triumph during this season.

Sagittarius, represented by the archer, occurs from November 22 – December 21. The planet Jupiter rules this season; it is the planet of abundance and growth and is the constellation of the zodiac that contains the center of the Milky Way. You really need Sagittarius' optimistic energy during this time of year when the veil is thin and you are conducting shadow work. This energy is also highly opinionated and wired to your belief system, which can challenge your inner work (ego mind versus subconscious). On the other hand, this energy can promote self-exploration for the purpose of deciding what you need to release as the collective moon energy begins to wane, which will positively change your current experience in this world. The archer that represents Sagittarius is a centaur, a half-human and half-horse creature, a learned healer whose higher intelligence forms a bridge between Earth and Heaven. The upward-shooting archer fixes its sight on the distant future, helping you to see your potential self and understand what you need to in order to move forward through your current experience. This fire sign represents personal transformation that is coming and welcomes change that magnetically attracts new opportunity.

Winter Solstice

The winter solstice occurs in Capricorn from December 22 – January 19 and is represented by the goat. This time of year is a catalyst of great resilience to endure the dark, long nights of winter and the frigid days before the Sun's radiance returns once again. It is a time for stillness that can best be spent resting and reflecting. This time of year represents the collective waning phase of the moon—when you want to let go of that which no longer serves you. Don't fear the upcoming and necessary surrender; doing so during this time of year can result in a deeply nourishing time in your life. This time of great darkness encourages you to spend time with loved ones and devote time to learning. While you may not typically sit around the fire while elders teach important lessons about life, there are many ways to learn. The beginning of Capricorn season brings the energy that makes you think of how you'd like to build and establish your legacy and how others will remember you before you shrug off the proverbial mortal coil. This establishment of self is reliant on releasing people, false beliefs, and tangible things from your life that negatively affect your story. You can't ignore this difficult aspect before you hunker down for winter and become cozy. Due to the spiritual and emotional nature of what Moon work collectively means for this time of year, people can become defensive and evasive. Also, during this time of year, Capricorn's sister sign, which is the energy of Cancer, may exemplify and heighten any psychic abilities you possess, which only serves to enhance your Moon work.

Winter solstice energy continues through Aquarius and Pisces. Aquarius, represented by the water bearer, occurs from January 20 – February 18. Filled with an energy that embraces individuality, the feeling of existing with limitless possibilities, and the propensity to transpire your personal capability to do anything, this energy makes people think that a "calendar" New Year is the optimal time to make a personal resolution. However, it is not a time for substantial changes, as the collective waning energy during this time of year doesn't support it. This is a time of questioning and exploring knowledge, increasing your spiritual awareness, and focusing on technological advances that you can use to help humanity. I write in general terms of "me" and "we" energy throughout this book, but this Aquarian energy is strongly related to energy outside of yourself—the collective "we" energy. In its highest expression, Aquarius energy is about discovering your authenticity and finding your true self (inner qualities) through developing innovative ideas (external learning and influence). This energy advocates for originality but also bringing your inner qualities out into the collective. There is nothing better for humanity than for unique individuals to live their truth and let their authentic nature shine! Think, "How can I embrace my inner humanitarian to move society forward by giving back to my community?" What you are giving to your community is yourself, your time, and your unique nature. This forward-focused energy creates the expectation of spending Aquarius season thinking about what the future holds. Saturn rules this water-bearer sign, bringing with it determination and responsibility. The water bearer is a human bringing forth water that represents life itself. The overreaching theme for this season is how we all as human beings can pour out our visions of a better and brighter future into the collective to make it so.

Pisces energy carries all the wisdom, experience, and energy of all the signs that came before it—karmic evolution. This time of year ends the cycle of the seasons, the Sun, and the moon—preparing us to begin a new cycle. Pisces, represented by the fish, occurs from February 19 – March 20. Collectively, the moon energy moves from the waning crescent to the dark moon. This energy is all about breaking down the barriers between your dreams and reality as you begin to wake from your winter slumber and look forward to spring. The symbolism of this sign is not only duality but also depth. As you dawn on the new beginnings of spring, the energy from this sign helps you find your hidden strengths, as well as discover any crutches you may be leaning on. Pisces, a water sign, is ruled by elusive Neptune—the planet of dreams, subconscious realms, spirituality, and compassion—helping you reflect on your year gone by, so remember... Leo season is representative of joy and your inner child, so did you play? How did you transform during Scorpio season? How did you encourage personal discipline during Capricorn season? As you contemplate your answers, start to dream about how you can do better for yourself and humanity for the next cycle of the seasons.

Everything is connected, and nothing is coincidence, so as the zodiac year comes to a close, use this time to see how much you've grown, evolved, and healed. But remember to always show yourself grace as you take this time to look in the mirror and truly see your lifetime of choices, experiences, and taught and learned beliefs to evaluate how they have affected you. Right now you are a combination of everything that has come before you in your experience. Start dreaming about what you want for your future experience and how it will transpire. One thing's for sure; the dreamy waters of Pisces embodied by the energy of fish are unique, colorful, and ver-satile. Never underestimate their power. We all came from the same divine place, and now it's time to gear up for the next period of new moon energy, prepare for spring, and discover what your soul craves.

You can see that each of these signs in the zodiac have different attributes that match up with lunar cycles. To better understand the uniqueness of each astrological sign and how to use its energy, you must look deeper at the sign's qualities, or its modes and modalities.

Modes (elements)

Earth has natural systems that are interconnected with one another, and, in and of itself, teaches you how to honor the elements. The four main elements are fire, air, earth, and water. While interpretations may differ, the overarching themes of balance, interconnectedness, and respect for nature are central to the understanding of the elements. I don't bring the fifth element of spirit into Wild Moon Healing because I believe that element to be the Earth's connection to Source. Just as you have a personal connection to your Source, this connection should reflect in the manner of your everyday living. Spirit is the immaterial element in all things, and the essential element that ties everything together to create balance or destroy it. To visualize the interconnectedness of the elements, imagine for a moment the game "rock, paper, scissors." From this perspective, see the way that an element can block, destroy, or eliminate the other. Air feeds fire, creating a brighter flame, and earth needs water to create life—expressing how the energy of modes empower one another. Too much air can cause a fire to spread out of control, and too much water can flood and erode the earth. From this vantage point you can see how the elements can be used in your Wild Moon Healing practice. A strong wind (i.e., an emotional experience or trauma) can blow out your inner spark or turn an empowering flame into raging, destructive emotions. Also, the earth (i.e., your foundation) can help you grow into the person you want to be, so long as you properly water your needs. We each have energetic qualities of the elements inside us, and just like everything else, they require balancing.

The energy of air keeps life moving and prevents stagnation. It symbolizes knowledge, perception, communication, creativity, and strategy. The air is representative of new beginnings, just as the Sun rises each day. Air therefore represents new moon energy and the season of spring, as well, and the cardinal direction of east. Air connects all the elements together, making it essential for life, as all living things require air to breathe and thrive. The energy of air is reminiscent of the circle of life, as it reminds us of the vast energetic network and how all energetic components stay connected. Air governs the mind and resides in the heart and throat chakras. While the energy of air is life itself, it can also destroy your energy. Think of an energetic vampire in the form of the Tasmanian Devil spinning out of control through your life, restricting access to your personal energy.

SPIRIT - Be * Connect * Listen * Know

FIRE	EARTH	AIR	WATER
Feel	Ground	Breathe	Cry
Ignite	Build	Observe	Flow
Transform	Heal	Resolve	Cleanse
Revise	Give	Focus	Release

Fire energy helps us discover our passion and build and maintain healthy boundaries. It symbolizes love, desire, anger, power, assertiveness, and raw energy. Fire is representative of eternity, birth, resurrection, hope, purification, and death, encompassing the entire cycle of life and the fullness of life. Fire also represents the waxing phases of the moon as it grows to fullness, the season of summer, and the cardinal direction of south. Fire governs the spirit and resides within your powerhouse, the solar plexus chakra. This energy is transformative because when merged with other elements, it can change and grow for your benefit or destruction. Think of a forest fire that erases all form of life; that same fire also transforms the landscape as new life begins to grow again. It is like The Tower card in tarot, which you should not fear because while what comes tumbling down can be jolting and life altering, on the other side of your experience lies transformation that can be exciting. When too much fire is in your life, you need to cleanse your energy.

Water energy is cleansing and helps facilitate necessary change. It symbolizes rebirth, healing, fertility, dreaming, clarity, and intuition. Through its healing qualities, water can bring clarity to emotions and heighten intuition. Water is symbolic for nourishment and holds profound significance in spiritual and esoteric practices. As water flows, it becomes a cleanser and purifier and is therefore related to the full moon, which metaphorically illuminates aspects of your shadow self that may require your attention. It's also associated with the cardinal direction of west, beautiful sunsets, and the season of autumn. When you harness the energy of water, you access its reflective and intuitive nature that can provide the guidance you need and seek from your Source and higher self. Think about the parable where Jesus turned water into wine—the essence of water is divine generosity! Water governs the soul and the essence of who you are, and therefore resides within the sacral chakra. While the energy of water is undoubtedly a calming and soothing element, too much of it can make you feel like you are drowning— bringing on bouts of depression, for example. When you feel overwhelmed, you need to ground your energy.

Earth energy keeps you grounded and rooted in your truth. It symbolizes stability, nourishment, security, fertility, health, and home life. The earth is the very foundation of life and abundance—it's where things grow and survive. The energy from Mother Earth is stable and fertile as she receives the "seeds" of other elements, as well as your own energy, and turns those divine gifts into abundance. The more time you spend in nature, the more your soul is organically nourished, which helps you find peace and a sense of home within. Representing the Great Mother, earth governs the body and resides within the root chakra. While earth is a principal element, the presence of the other elements is required to fully realize its power and capabilities. Just as Pisces' energy encompasses the combined nature of all that came before it—because without a beginning there cannot exist a culmination of a cycle—the element of earth encompasses all the other elemental energy, because it would not exist without air, water, or fire.

Elements and Zodiac Attributes

Above we talked about the four different elements, but now let us correlate the attributes of each element to the energy of the corresponding zodiac signs. There are four zodiac elements (earth, air, fire, water), with three zodiac signs belonging to each element group. The elements are interchangeably called "triplicities" because there are three signs per element. When you look at your birth chart, the elements of your Sun, moon, and rising signs are of significant importance, but the overall distribution of elements in your chart is what counts the most. Having more than four planets in a single element will have an impact on your behavior, even if that element does not correspond to your Sun sign. Ultimately, the elements are a life-giving source of energy for the twelve zodiac signs. The importance of personally understanding the elements is so you may better understand yourself. If any of the qualities listed below are something you want to grow in your life, then energetically work with that particular element and zodiac to strengthen that characteristic in yourself. You are not limited to only working with the element associated with your Sun sign.

Air signs are Gemini, Libra, and Aquarius. This energy favors mental action such as thinking, learning, and communication. This energy is about sharing information, interacting with others, and influencing society. When the winds die down, stagnant energy can create boredom. As a Libra, I know that being bored is the worst thing for me, as I may have a tendency to find trouble, albeit harmless fun. These zodiac signs are master communicators, socializers, and attention seekers, and they are curious. People owning the qualities of these signs are adventurous multitaskers who like to take everything in through observance. Since each sign is unique, they use the energy of air differently. Gemini energy is intellectually curious whereas Libra and Aquarius energies are focused on relationships. Libra energy is partnership driven while Aquarius energy is friendship based. When you find a purpose, Aquarian energy can make you unstoppable. Positive attributes of air energy include being articulate, objective, mentally clear, understanding, socially adaptable, cooperative, relational, and capable of forethought. Those not in tune with this energy may be unemotional, lacking in sympathy, impractical, disassociated from the body and the physical world, over-adaptive, or hyperactive.

Fire signs are Aries, Leo, and Sagittarius. This energy favors action, responds quickly, conquers, leads, and loves to travel. These signs will take risks and love new adventures. These signs are confident, idealistic, and intense, providing you what you need to approach life with zest and enthusiasm. Common traits of these zodiac signs include being passionate, aggressive, spontaneous, impulsive, and courageous. People owning the qualities of these signs cannot be dominated; they take risks and turn opportunities to their favor. But each sign is unique—Aries energy takes action, Leo energy leads grandly, and Sagittarius energy takes on exploration of the unknown. When you think of the element of fire and the zodiac signs under this element, the positive characteristics include being extroverted, energetic, enthusiastic, inspirational, visionary, high-spirited, direct, physically active, courageous, and warm. Those not in tune with this energy may be overly active to the point of burnout, lack perspective, and experience restlessness, impatience, selfishness, insensitivity, willfulness, hastiness, thoughtlessness, impulsivity, recklessness, and extravagance.

Water signs are Cancer, Scorpio, and Pisces. The moon and water are soul mates, considering their reflective qualities and influence over tides. This energy is intuitive, responding to outside energy almost unconsciously. These zodiac signs tend to be extremely emotional yet calm and sensitive yet sharp. People owning the qualities of these signs will do anything to avoid confrontation. The energy of water is deeply emotional and portrays itself differently in each sign. Cancer energy is the most emotional of all signs, seeking to nurture or be nurtured. Scorpio acts with laser-focused passion and intense vision. Pisces energy is more difficult to describe, as its energy is chameleon-like, absorbing its surroundings. Positive attributes of this energy are being deeply emotional, sympathetic, empathetic, nurturing, calm, peaceful, sensitive, compassionate, imaginative, intuitive, and psychically aware. When this energy is out of balance within you, you may take things personally and get your feelings hurt easily. Those not in tune with water energy may be emotionally insecure and unstable, shy, timid, lacking in confidence, oversensitive, easily influenced and manipulated, withdrawn, uncommunicative, vindictive, vengeful, moody, or depressed.

Earth signs are Taurus, Virgo, and Capricorn. This energy is more cautious, practical, and realistic, because of the need to ground and obtain good footing before moving on. This dependable, thorough, and solid energy needs a vision, a plan, and an organized structure. These zodiac signs are typically practical, reliable, logical, and grounded. People owning the qualities of these signs are responsible, hardworking, and loyal—working hard to find solutions to problems as they occur. Each sign possesses unique qualities of this element; Taurus energy ponders things to create vision, Virgo energy will analyze to create a plan, and Capricorn energy will work the plan based on the created structure. When you think of the element of earth and the zodiac signs under this element, the positive characteristics include being practical, efficient, organized, realistic, patient, self-disciplined, diligent, productive, enduring, persistent, dependable, and stable and having good common sense. When this energy is out of balance, you may feel slow or heavy—your entire life may be in a state of stagnation. Those not in tune with this energy may lack vision, or be unimaginative, petty, excessively conventional, narrow-minded, stubborn, or resistant to change.

After you have knowledge of the elements and how their energy works under each zodiac sign, you have to go deeper to figure out what qualities gives each sign its uniqueness.

Modalities (qualities)

Zodiac qualities indicate how people respond to stimuli, and especially how they act under tension. This energy indicates how the signs express the energy of the corresponding element, meaning the behavior used to express the element's needs. There are three qualities: cardinal, fixed, and mutable. They are also called "quadruplicities" because there are four signs per group. To maintain balance, all energy has attributes of feminine (heavy) or masculine (light); yin (-) or yang (+); extroverted and self-expressive or introverted and receptive; and active or passive. All of these archetype qualities are necessary in every individual for balance, regardless of sex or gender. Strength is not just physical but emotional as well. Divine feminine energy is heavier because it is emotional, internal, and reflective. The negative polarity of yin energy makes it more receptive, passive, and introverted. This is the type of energy necessary to go inward and find the truth of who you are. The lighter divine masculine energy deeply connects to your internal warrior, doing physical things, and experiencing adventures. The positive polarity of yang energy is active, extroverted, and self-expressive. This is the energy of expressing your authentic nature to the outside world.

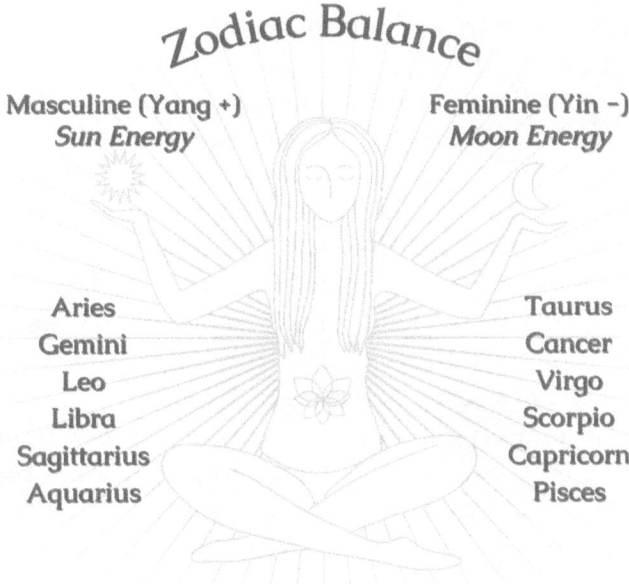

Zodiac Balance

Masculine (Yang +)
Sun Energy

Feminine (Yin −)
Moon Energy

Aries	Taurus
Gemini	Cancer
Leo	Virgo
Libra	Scorpio
Sagittarius	Capricorn
Aquarius	Pisces

Positive and negative energy of each sign is not indicative of energetic forces such as good versus bad or divine versus evil. It's more about chemistry, such as how protons, neutrons, and electrons create all the unique elements on the periodic table. There aren't protons binding to neutrons to create unique zodiac energies; rather, positive and negative reflect polarity or opposing zodiac signs, which balance each other. You can use all of these words interchangeably. So, feminine, female, negative, passive, introverted, indirect, and receptive are all words that describe yin energy, also known as feminine energy. Likewise, masculine, male, positive, extroverted, direct, and active are words that describe yang energy, also known as masculine energy. Air and fire signs are yang energy and go with each other, while earth and water signs are yin energy and go with each other. These attributes divide the zodiac into two groups of feminine and masculine energy, thus creating balance. But to point out what makes each zodiac sign distinctive, we have to go more in depth than just balance.

Adding qualities to the balancing attributes provides each zodiac with its uniqueness. The qualities are either cardinal, fixed, or mutable. Cardinal modality is reflective of new beginnings, as each of the cardinal zodiac signs usher in a new season (spring, summer, fall, and winter). This energy is assertive and initiates change. These signs are big thinkers who are excellent at brainstorming and initiating but may lack follow-through. So, the behavior to engage the elemental energy results in starting new things. This energy is about self-starting on projects, but also in a crisis, this energy becomes motivated. Each sign uses this energy differently. Aries energy, the only cardinal sign with the energy of fire, seeks leadership and control in general, and those with this energy are decisive and move on with confidence and courage. Cancer energy, the only cardinal sign with the energy of water, seeks to control the areas of emotions, home, and family, moving in a very methodical way. Libra energy, the only cardinal sign with the element of air, tries to control partnerships and move with a balanced approach to planning. Capricorn energy, the only cardinal sign with the energy of earth, tries to control, use, and exploit the material environment through hard work but moves in a more cautious and realistic way.

Fixed modality sustains the current energy of the season, digging in its heels, as each of the fixed zodiac signs come in the middle of each season. This energy is stable and self-contained. The behavior to engage the elemental energy is passive, yet it is determined, unwavering, and stubborn. The quality of this energy is consistency, and even loyalty. This energy manages and sustains what began under the cardinal energy that preceded it. Change is always occurring, so if you are out of balance with this energy, you may go into denial in the face of change, or be resistant to change altogether, which is why people with a fixed Sun sign may tend to be late or refuse to leave a job that is making them ill. Each sign uses this energy differently. The passive nature of Taurus, the only fixed sign with the element of earth, is just slow because of its pragmatic nature toward planning. Scorpio, the only fixed sign with the element of water, uses tardiness as a subtle power struggle because of their determined yet passive nature. The determination of Leo, the only fixed sign with the element of fire, enjoys making an entrance because they are so aware of their duty that they go about things in a bold and enthusiastic manner. Aquarius energy, the only fixed sign with the element of air, wants things on its own terms because this energy is disciplined, serious, and mature, giving an air of expertise in handling all situations.

Mutable modality loosens structures to prepare for changing conditions to come, as each of the mutable zodiac signs occur in months that transition into the next season. The unstable nature of this shifting energy makes it most open to influence by the environment. The behavior to engage the elemental energy is transition or adaptability— move from the old to the new, and as such, makes way for the energy of the next cardinal sign. This energy is flexible and tolerant due to its nature and its ability to easily let things go. If this energy is out of balance, you may be prone to worry with much rattling about in your head, but without tangible form your thoughts may begin to anticipate negative outcomes. Try not to worry, as the strength of this energy is adaptability, so you won't agonize for long. Each sign uses this energy differently. Gemini energy, the only mutable sign with the element of air, has an influence to change your ideas, as they are adaptable, conscious, and quite helpful. Virgo energy, the only sign with the element of earth, changes or influences by the direction of its environment because the energy is intelligent, dedicated, and committed. Sagittarius energy, the only mutable sign with the element of fire, has a continually changing view of life's possibilities, so this energy is more adaptable and determined. Pisces energy, the only mutable sign with the element of water, adapts itself superficially to its environment (like a chameleon) and reflects it like a mirror, because of its still nature that is sensitive, receptive, and compassionate.

	Fire	Earth	Air	Water
Cardinal	Aries	Capricorn	Libra	Cancer
Fixed	Leo	Taurus	Aquarius	Scorpio
Mutable	Sagittarius	Virgo	Gemini	Pisces

There are three signs under each element, but only one of them can be cardinal, fixed, or mutable. The combination of elements, attributes, and qualities associated with each sign is what provides its uniqueness and creates polarity. If you compromise so much that you sacrifice your own interest and the truth of who you are, you are in need of balance. The best way to learn about energy balance is through polarity.

Polarity

Each zodiac sign has a relationship with its partner on the exact opposite side of the zodiac wheel, known as its sister sign. In astrology, the term polarity expresses this fact. All energies are necessary for balanced energetic flow, which comes in the form of a new or full moon. Each of the twelve signs of the zodiac mirror natural rules considering several aspects: the primordial qualities—the basis of everything; the modes/elements (air, fire, water, and earth); the modalities (yin/yang and quality of cardinal, fixed, or mutable); the polarities; and the planets. Understanding these basic zodiac qualities can help you grasp how each Sun sign acts differently regarding new and full moon energy.

These polarities help you understand how to use this energy to learn more about yourself—heal, transform, and navigate life month by month. The energy field of action is not watertight, as the distinct types of energy interact with and complement each other. Opposite signs share a modality, so they are more similar than you would think, but they are always of different elements (see modes section), so they can work together to create either balance or conflict. For example, Aries polarity is Libra. Both are cardinal signs with leadership qualities, but Aries is a fire sign, so it leads in more of a physical way, whereas Libra is an air sign and as such, prefers freedom in the form of thought. Aries energy prefers conflict, while Libra seeks peace. In the end, both signs can benefit from one another—Aries could use a little more tact, while Libra could use a little more passion. When you are in the season of Libra, reflect back to the spring to see what's come to fruition—do you need a little more tact or more passion as you chase your intention or big dream for your life? Conduct this type of analysis every month against the zodiac sign six months prior to help deepen your level of growth and transformation.

For purposes of Wild Moon Healing, I like to think of polarity as "me" verses "we" energy. For example, how do I use more tact or passion (as with the Aries/Libra polarity example above) to bring my true self into the collective (we energy)? There is an energy inside of you which contains everything you can control (me energy). Then there is independent energy in your environment, including the collective energy of society that is outside of your control (we energy). The only way to influence the collective, or bring your true self into society, is by being authentic. You become more authentic as you progress with your Moon work. Each of the polarities in the zodiac work together to create new and full moon energy necessary to create balance. Later we'll explore the energy of each zodiac sign and how its energy changes depending on whether the sign is a new or full moon. But first let's take a deeper look at the energy of each sign and what creates unique personality traits in different people born under that sign.

3

LUNAR INFLUENCES

Full and New Moon Energetic Influences

When the Sun and moon are both in the same zodiac sign, that gives us a new moon. The polarity created when the Sun and moon oppose each other gives us a full moon. New and full moon energy can be felt up to three days before and after their specific alignment. The actual new moon occurs at the precise moment in time when the Sun and the moon are directly aligned in the sky. The actual full moon occurs at the precise moment in time when the Sun and the moon oppose each other. The energy of a new moon launches a new cycle of light—new beginnings. It's a cosmic reset button that you can access at the beginning of every lunar cycle. If you are looking for a restart, the energy that supports beginnings, setting intentions, and planting seeds for future growth occurs under a new moon. Full moon energy is about harvesting what you've been working on during the waxing phase of the moon, but it also sheds light on your metaphorical path so you can see things more clearly. The opposition of the Sun and moon create an unstable atmosphere, with the ultimate goal of finding balance through each sign in the zodiac. It is difficult for you to grow and transform your life if everything is handed to you. Nature understands this fact, so it structures imbalance and sometimes chaos to shake things up, wake you up, and challenge you to become better than you were before. Polarity of the Sun and moon helps to shift your awareness and consciousness. Connecting to these energies grounds you to create a sense of stability in your life and provides you with a sense of direction.

When you don't connect to these energies, you lack a sense of direction. Someone may even describe you as a lunatic! The word "lunacy" comes from the moon because in ancient times people believed in the mind-altering power of La Luna. The universe's intention with full moon energy is not to fill emergency rooms and put a higher demand on law enforcement to keep the peace. Individuals who are not living authentically, from a place of love, and don't know how to harness this energy create these situations whether they realize it or not. When your intention is to work directly with new and full moon energy, you gain balance and revelations in your conscious mind while strengthening your connection with lunar (and all) energy to help align your internal energetic network to include chakras. So, while shadow work under a full moon may seem daunting and scary, know that your path to kindness and forgiveness is activated during Moon work, making the time of the full moon the perfect time to identify what negativity you need to release. Letting something go creates space for new things and also brings balance to your personal energy system. You must be in tune with the energy represented by each new and full moon as a force to reckon with your inner self, which you can connect to through inner child work or trauma healing.

To ultimately shift your perspective, new moon energy helps you create an actual path or plan to follow, while full moon energy illuminates your metaphorical path, bridging the gap between your conscious mind and your soul, if you are willing to listen. You have all the answers you seek inside of you. Use this energy to strengthen your intuition and recognize injustice inside of you so you can heal. New moon energy helps to highlight your strengths with encouraging energy. Whereas, full moon energy brings imbalances and challenges to the surface, which is why people not engaging in Moon work seem to go mad under a full moon—they are, in fact, lunatics.

A trick to see how working with the new and full moons will affect a particular area of your life is to check your natal chart. For example, under a Libra moon, see which house Libra falls in on your chart. For instance, if Libra is in your First House, it will influence your health and vitality. This energy is not just for full or new moons; as the moon is the

fastest moving heavenly body in the sky, it moves through all the signs of the zodiac every month. If you are in need of some Taurean energy to work on your finances like you are a bull on Wall Street, just use an app to find out when the moon is in Taurus each month so you can work on that energy during those particular days. As you read the information below, remember that everything is connected, so planets and other energetic and celestial factors will affect these basic definitions of how energy works with the moon.

Aries

Aries is a cardinal fire sign that rules the First House of *the self*—who you are inside and out. If you do a tarot spread under each moon, you can pull out The Emperor as a signifier of this energy. Aries is ruled by the assertive planet Mars, which pushes the agenda toward bold action, standing up for yourself, and initiating change. Courage and instinct are favored under this sign, so use "I am" mantras to help embrace this energy. This astrological sign is a born leader that uses masculine energy to move forthrightly with vigor. This energy could quickly detonate into a conflict though, so be cautious. Ram energy will head-butt its way through anything without being overly concerned about the outcome.

When there's a new moon in Aries, a phase which happens around the equinox in March, and marks the beginning of the astrological year when the Sun and moon are both in Aries, there's no better time to take a new idea and put it into motion by planting metaphorical seeds of intention or creating a solid goal. With its raw and primal energy, Aries is bursting with enthusiasm, courage, and passion. Both the new moon in Aries and the Sun sign of Aries signify a time of rebirth and new beginnings that can electrify your nervous system. This intensity can either fuel your passions or cause you to feel frustrated, and you may run out of mojo. Allow any feelings to boil to the surface so you can work through them and release any negative emotions, allowing you to shift into a more productive mode. If you haven't already started planning your year ahead, during the Aries new moon you will want to revisit *every* intention, goal, or dream you have for your life. As you experience a desire to take manageable, action-oriented steps toward your goals, make sure they align with your soul's purpose. The energetic vibration of Aries is explosive and can propel you into the next level of your personal evolution when harnessed and directed.

The full moon in Aries occurs around the equinox in September when the Sun is in Libra. Rather than wanting to plant the seeds of intentions as you did in March, this is the time of year when you want to harvest the energy of what you planted six months ago during the new moon in Aries. Look back on your journaling to see how far you've come. A full moon in Aries aligns with your mission in life; whether you will see your hard work come to fruition or not depends on the level of effort you've been putting in toward your goal. If there is nothing to harvest, then you may be working toward the wrong goal, using unrealistic action steps, or need to heal spiritually, mentally, or physically before you can realistically achieve the goal(s) you've set for yourself. If so, this is the time of year to plant seeds for balance to help you achieve your goals. Since Aries rules the head, you may want to take time to relax and meditate to still your mind. If there is conflict in doing so, Aries may want you to feed your head instead, so direct any uneasy energy toward learning to create stillness.

Taurus

Taurus is a fixed earth sign full of feminine energy, as it's ruled by Venus. Associated with the Second House of money and value of material things, Taurus represents the energy of practicality and stability—two sensations that will become increasingly important when the new moon is in Taurus. This sign's energy can help stabilize your energy, as it is graced with grounding earth energy. Due to its ruling planet, this sign will always relate to great taste and pleasurable pastimes. However, this energy can make people behave as "stubborn as a bull" or to a drastic extreme, such as acting like a "bull in a china shop." When you are tapped into this energy, you're aware of how you are steady, grounded, practical, and reliable. You can feel safe using Taurus energy to weather any storm at a consistent pace.

The new moon in Taurus occurs in mid-spring when the Sun is in the sign of Taurus. This new moon encourages grounded energy and a connection with nature, but take the "Taurus" approach, which is slow and easy. So, plant seeds of connection during this time. Aries energy was about finding your groove and establishing a goal, but now you want to put in real effort, start networking, and examine the possible rewards your effort will bring. Consolidate Aries' energy of a spark into a form with more substance by focusing on self-improvement and replacing negative habits with positive ones that will help you grow and shift your energy. An energetic shift results in the proverbial "a-ha" moment when you make a connection between two seemingly different things. New moon energy under this sign may bring up issues around safety and comfort. Make note that accumulating things as a means of feeling safe could be you substituting self-worth for possessions. The biggest question under Taurus new moon energy is, "Does this support my life?" This question helps aid you by encouraging spring cleaning and decluttering. Accountability is the overreaching energetic theme. Use this energy to figure out what's good for you. If you are unbalanced, you may feel disconnected from the physical world and may be unable to say the word *no* to create safe and healthy boundaries in your life.

The full moon in Taurus occurs when the Sun is in Scorpio, around mid-autumn. These energies—the intricacies of Scorpio season and simplistic Taurus energy—counterbalance each other. The full moon in Taurus can be used to stimulate feelings of rebirth, breakthroughs, and a desire to surrender to negative impulsiveness. It can be an exciting but unpredictable energy. Pay close attention to all of your senses—specifically what you can touch, taste, smell, and feel. Use your senses to ground yourself and make life simple again. Those not connected to this energy may seem to act abrasively. Remember you cannot control anything outside of yourself, and be sure to choose who you share your energy with wisely.

Gemini

Gemini is a mutable air sign ruled by Mercury, the planet of communication, and is associated with the Third House of communication. The energy from Gemini is both versatile and scattered—it's hard to focus your attention on one thing because something else always shows up to break your concentration, plus there is a natural curious nature of this energy. All of its buzzing about is not for naught because this energy helps you to capture your environment and responds immediately before moving on to the next thing that catches your attention. With its focus on communication, this energy has the ability to influence your relationships, career, and even self-expression. Geminis have a restless nature that requires downtime to rejuvenate, so if you feel the need for a break, make sure you honor yourself. This energy is a nonconformist who adapts to new situations quickly but then disappears just as fast, leaving others wondering what happened. The duality of this energy allows you to deliberately change your mind about something, especially if it is something you've been fixated on for a while—change is the name of its game.

The new moon is always a cosmic turning point—it's when we say goodbye to one cycle and hello to the next one. At the end of spring, around May, the Sun and the moon will both be in the sign of Gemini, making it a new moon. This is the time to really plant some metaphorical seeds of change. You don't need to know how something will happen or unfold—how could you possibly have prior knowledge of that anyway? Even with heightened intuition, the universe loves to surprise us. As with all new moons, be sure to release the outcome of your new moon intention so you can be open to any opportunity that comes your way. Gemini energy can make you feel restless and make it hard to follow through, so you don't want to work on every little detail of your intention right now anyway. Let the seeds of your intention take their own shape and allow the universe to take the reins. Mercury's influence on this new moon encourages socialization and asks you to approach new avenues of self-expression and creativity.

Six months later, at the end of autumn, the Sun will be in Sagittarius while the moon is in Gemini, giving us a full moon. Look back at the seeds you planted at the end of spring to see how they have manifested. Have you created the change you needed to succeed? Sagittarius is not easily distracted, but the jittery energy from the Gemini full moon can result in your mind trying to focus on a million minor details all at once. This is not the time to create new change. Nervous tension, anxiety, and stress could be problems for you under this energy. Roll up your sleeves and use this energy to submerge yourself into your current project, or better yet, put it into your own personal transformation. Gemini energy can affect your nervous system and make you come across as a bundle of nervous energy because you are intellectualizing your feelings in an attempt to articulate them. Sharing emotions is hard for anyone to do. As you perform shadow work under this full moon, Mercury's influence wants you to share information, so find someone you trust to talk out your moods with—or journal if you don't have the right person in your life for this. If you notice jittery mental energy worsening when you are still, change things up by doing something new, or at least do something differently than you are doing right now.

Cancer

Cancer is a cardinal water sign that ushers in summer. The moon rules Cancer, so this sign is the epitome of moon child energy, or having a deep connection to the moon and reverence for the divine feminine reflected in nature and within. This energy is about who you were (younger/past self) and who you are now. Under the Cancer influence you may feel more sensitive and vulnerable than you do during other times of the year. Cancer energy is associated with the Fourth House of home and family. This mothering and intuitive energy (think divine feminine and Mother Earth) brings out our nurturing qualities of domesticity, sympathy, sensitiveness, and protectiveness. Emotions will be heightened during a Cancer moon, and it's easy to become moody, touchy, or restless if you don't express how you're feeling. Typically, this energy makes you feel most comfortable being authentic around your family or your closest friends.

In the early summer when the moon and Sun are both in the sign of Cancer, we have a new moon in Cancer. Tap into the psychological need of this sign to give and receive warmth and security, which will help you show empathy and compassion for others. This energy makes it easier to understand where those around you are coming from on an emotional level. Since this energy is protective and tends to hold things in, use the new moon to plant metaphorical seeds for what you keep hidden. Those dreams you are afraid to say anything about need a chance to grow, so sow them with intention. Also, this energy urges you to explore your self-care routines and build new rituals that lift your vibrations and encourage intuition since this energy tends to be overemotional.

Six months later, at the beginning of winter, when the Sun is in the sign of Capricorn, we have a full moon in Cancer. As you would think, Capricorn energy is very much different than the polarity of Cancer. Capricorn is all about the outside world, and as we now know, Cancer is emotional and inwardly comforting and protective. These energies help counterbalance each other by bringing fruition to those things you held close under the Cancer new moon. You know, the stuff you were afraid to tell anyone about. You can finally manifest those things with a sense of safety and security as you bring your feelings out into the open. This is a great time to get introspective and explore your emotions, learning more about your needs and desires. While emotions may be overwhelming, there are many things you can do to comfort yourself, like yoga and meditation.

Leo

The ruler of this fixed, fiery, theatrical sign is the Sun. Leo is a feisty, social sign that encourages us to embrace the simple joys of being alive. Being associated with the Fifth House of pleasure reinforces that Leo energy is all about you—your interests, creative self-expression, and even your love affairs. Just like a lion, this sign is about being big-hearted and loyal. You can use this energy to express your feelings in a healthy manner, such as letting people know you love them, and express appreciation with ease. Leos crave attention, so the energy under this sign could make you feel insecure and result in a dramatic flare-up. So, make sure you express love to yourself as well by celebrating and accepting all of yourself!

During mid-summer, when the Sun and moon are in the sign of Leo, we have what is called a Leo new moon. This new moon is concerned with creating, self-expression, and showing what's in your heart, so plant seeds of intention to create something great in your life. Use this generous energy to increase your ability to accept yourself for who you are and explore your creative nature. In doing so you will cultivate the confidence you need to share your gifts and talents with the world. Because there is only one of you, take this time to practice gratitude for your unique personality and vision. Just remember, this lion energy requires you to open your heart so you can manifest your deepest desires into reality. This is a great time to ask yourself if you've truly been doing the things that make you feel the most fulfilled.

Six months later, when the Sun is in the sign of Aquarius and the moon is in Leo, we experience a Leo full moon. Aquarius is cold and distant and ruled by disruptive Uranus, so Leo's bright energy helps to balance that out. Be careful that the abrasive nature of Aquarius' ruling planet doesn't make you act in a way that is arrogant, overbearing, or obstinate. Aquarius and Leo energy are both independent but express that differently, causing some confrontation. Leo is independent in the way it seeks and experiences personal pleasure, just being you with no regard to anything outside of you, while Aquarius uses its liberated energy to be you within the collective "we" energy. This transit helps you feel okay to acknowledge what is in your heart. When you can acknowledge what is in your heart, taking bold heart-centered actions are favored. You may feel more flirtatious when the full moon is hanging out in Leo, making this an exciting time to put yourself out there. Before you do, put your vanity and false pride in check.

Virgo

Virgo is a mutable earth sign ruled by Mercury. This energy of inner communication and order may make you want to organize and declutter your living space. Its practical energy works with Mercury's influence on having an active mind. Curiosity killed the cat as they say, but that doesn't stop this energy, who is intent on getting to the good stuff. Its analytical nature craves more information. You can leave it to Virgo energy to figure out what's useful or useless, what's true or untrue, or what's right or wrong. It's not surprising that this sign's motto is "I analyze." Virgos love to pitch in and pay close attention to detail, so tap into those traits when the moon is in Virgo. Also, since Virgo energy is associated with your Sixth House of health, use this energy to take your health more seriously as well.

In the late summer, when the Sun and the moon are both in the sign of Virgo, you experience what is called a Virgo new moon. Virgo gives you the ability to analyze any situation and find solutions for your problems, and ultimately reach a place of balance. This new moon is different because you are not planting any seeds; rather, you are figuring out what to do with your harvest. The lingering question is, "Where do I go from here?" This energy will help you figure out how you can tangibly or tactfully utilize what you've been working on to create something bigger. This energy does help you multitask, so you don't have to focus on just one thing. This is also a great time to evaluate your self-care routines. Use this influence to make to-do lists, tackle chores, and embrace little accomplishments.

Six months later, at the end of winter, you experience what is known as a Virgo full moon. The Sun is in Pisces at this time, so you may be lost in thought, dreaming about tomorrow. Allow Virgo energy to bring a sense of grounding to help show you that you can turn your dreams into reality.

When it comes to shadow work, focus on eliminating the habits and patterns of behavior that don't serve you physically. As you remove things from your life, remember the perfectionist energy of Virgo brings attention to health. Don't let any illusion or delusion of your health from Pisces energy cause you to overlook yourself from a physical perspective. As Virgo fears disease, hopefully this energy will have you stop and consider how your habits, behaviors, and hygiene affect your health.

Libra

This cardinal air sign ushers in fall and the energy of change. As you experience the amazing color transformation that autumn gifts you every single year, without fail, its impartial energy reminds you that change is good, necessary, and beautiful, and not to fear it. This energy is associated with the Seventh House of partnerships and embodies how you love. Libra energy uses love to create balance—and it doesn't just appreciate balance; it seeks it out. When a hurdle finds itself in the way of a Libra, they just dance around it, like they knew it was there all along. The dance you create helps you to find balance again. Libra's energy works hard to make you think you are the master of moving on. Because Libra's natural skills are diplomacy and negotiation, the moon in Libra gives you the ability to use charm and tact to get what you want.

When the Sun and moon are in Libra, you experience the Libra new moon. The new moon in Libra is all about planting seeds to reestablish balance and self-preservation that has been lost by the eventful obligations of summer. Balance is a peaceful neutral point where common sense and cooperation come from. This energy helps you see both sides to a story on a personal level. Libra energy will want you to hit the emotional reset button so you can look at your horizon with new anticipation. If you're not balanced, some opportunity in your future may be out of view. During any moon in Libra, you may struggle with getting your point across when speaking authentically. You will want to work with your throat chakra if this is the case.

Full moons are all about duality, and the social grace of a Libra full moon is no exception, as it challenges you to manage your desire for companionship with your need for independence. This moon occurs when the Sun is in Aries, so Libra takes this strong sense of "me" energy, and you must see how you can blend it with "we" energy of relationships or partnerships. Ask yourself: "How can I show up in this situation, relationship, or society in general and remain truly authentic?" Maintaining or creating self-preservation tactics is important during this full moon. Harness this energy to show off your inner charm but remember sometimes it's more about delivery than the actual message. If you lack poise, you may tip the scales, creating a volatile or unstable atmosphere.

Scorpio

This fixed water sign is ruled by the transformation planet, Pluto. This energy is mysterious and passionate. If what ignites your passion is in question, you may react sharply and with that stinger Scorpio is known for. Passion may also imply that you can go to extremes with your actions and emotions. A Scorpio moon is not low-key because it is associated with the Eighth House of transformation. In times of crisis, this energy and the energy of Pluto help empower you to adapt, evolve, and take control. Due to the time of year of the Sun sign in Scorpio, this energy is introspective and could lead to greater self-awareness, as well as awareness to aspects of your physical environment.

Use this energy to understand the depth of your feelings and gain and better understanding of what drives your passions.

New moons are times of planting seeds, and the Scorpio new moon urges us to plant the seed of expression and transformation. Too bad the ruling plant isn't Mercury, but that would make things too easy. It is hard to speak your truth in a healthy manner, especially when your truth is in direct conflict with others. You may feel torn between helping yourself and providing help to others. How do you know when your need is greater than that of someone else? As long as you express yourself from the heart as best you can, you won't get lost in comparing your needs to others, because that is a losing battle. You will not only have a strong need to express your feelings, but you will also experience your feelings more deeply. Powerful and profound Scorpio doesn't hold anything back, and it is very resourceful! Just know that the greatest treasures are found when you are willing to delve deep into your feelings.

The full moon in emotionally intense Scorpio is always a dynamic event. There is always a tug of war due to the polarity of the signs. In this case the war is between practical Taurus and enthusiastic Scorpio. These energies counterbalance each other by helping you see what you really need in your life and what needs to go. This energy can rock your relationships and finances, but trust the universe ultimately knows what's best for you. Conflict during the Scorpio full moon creates opportunity for positive breakthroughs by eliminating bad habits, behaviors, or people from your life. You could be the one eliminated from someone's life if you exhibit the negative side of Scorpios' energy (i.e., uncompromising, hot tempered, vindictive, resentful, jealous, or envious). Whichever way you sway, this energy can be intense.

Sagittarius

Sagittarius is a mutable fire sign and is ruled by Jupiter, the planet of luck. This energy is much welcomed after any Scorpio energy, as it is optimistic, philosophical, and adventurous. It is associated with the Ninth House, which encompasses traveling and learning new things so you can broaden your mind, which is the only way to discover your purpose in life. Those of you who are more pragmatic and cynical (which is an energetic leak) may even find yourself a little more optimistic when this energy comes around. Roadblocks and obstacles in life are no match for all the possibilities your mind can muster. Your thoughts could lead you into uncharted waters—how exciting! When a new adventure presents itself, go for it.

The Sagittarius new moon asks you to plant the seeds of optimism. When you create your intention under this new moon, try to include space by leaving painful parts of your past behind so you can visualize a better future. The past is the past; you can't live there, and trying to do so will only ruin your present moment and thus your future. It is not always plausible to remove yourself from your present circumstance, but the loyal energy of this new moon brings hope and all the wonderful things that go with the concept of faith. Don't see your situation for what it is, rather how it could be. Spiritual activities and studying are favored under this influence—it's the time to open your mind and let new ideas and higher vibrations penetrate your aura.

A full moon in Sagittarius is an interesting time, because the moon in far-seeing Sagittarius opposes the Sun in nearsighted Gemini. Funny enough, the motto for this energy is "I see." This is a time when you may be overwhelmed with ideas and information, but this full moon counterbalances Gemini energy by helping you focus your attention on long-term, big-picture goals, rather than wallowing in the details.

The over-confident, blunt, dogmatic, and exaggerated nature of this energy could create issues for you. Be careful with your finances. Jupiter's generosity wants to shower you with blessings and abundance, making this an overly optimistic transit. Just remember the risks of activities such as gambling—let the universe bring you miracles, rather than attempting to create them yourself. The overreaching psychological need of Sagittarius energy is to explore and expand horizons. So don't ask, "Why?" under this moon; instead ask, "Why not?"

Capricorn

Capricorn is ruled by Saturn, associated with both the root and crown chakras—the beginning and the end. Saturn relates to the trials and tribulations that you experience in your life, how you react or respond to your situation, and also the ultimate resolution of karma. Under Capricorn's diplomatic and goal-oriented nature, you tend to be a little more cautious, reserved, and careful, and serious due to Saturn's influence. Capricorn is a sign that is responsible because it appreciates hard work, focus, and determination. It's not surprising that this energy is associated with the Tenth House of enterprise, but without Saturn's influence you wouldn't be able to achieve your goal. As an earth sign, this energy helps you with a shot of determination to achieve whatever it is you set your mind to.

A Capricorn new moon is like the beginning of a brand-new personal year. Most people make New Year's resolutions during this time of year, but the collective energy doesn't support that. However, professionally speaking, the ambitious Capricorn energy provides you with enough patience, discipline, and persistence to reach the top. This energy also needs structure and social acknowledgment.

Under this new moon energy, you can't help but focus on your career goals or legacy and concentrate on the work it will take to move closer to success. As you plant seeds of resilience, it's a great time to create a new budget or plan to move towards your dreams.

During the time the moon in Capricorn faces the Sun in Cancer, you experience the Capricorn full moon. Both signs are associated with security, yet conflict arises in the way they each seek it out. Capricorn is concerned with accomplishments and external status, while the desire of Cancer is to find comfort and safety internally through your feelings. These energies counterbalance by helping you to choose a hard or soft approach to your situation. Ask yourself: "How can I be tough in a sensitive situation and sensitive in a tough situation?" Don't abandon your feelings; rather, learn to compartmentalize. When you master this dance, you feel at home inside yourself and in the world around you. A full moon in Capricorn provides you with energy that works even harder to help you finish what you started at the beginning of the lunar cycle. "No" is a full and complete sentence; it identifies that you have given enough, and it's a perfectly good response that sets boundaries so you don't take on too many responsibilities. However, Capricorn energy doesn't like to take no for an answer regarding career and professional advancement. This prideful energy can cause suspicion, selfishness, pessimism, and deceitful natures to arise. The motto of this energy is "I use," so use this energy wisely to help you tackle any obstacle.

Aquarius

Aquarius is a fixed air sign ruled by Uranus, which is disruptive, erratic, and revolutionary, only because it represents the unconscious urge to find your individuality. It seeks to find what is in the greater good for humanity and goes about it in the spirit of chaos. Aquarius energy is quirky, humanitarian, and independent. This altruistic energy helps you march to the beat of your own drum; you cannot put an Aquarian in a box. Aquarius is my rising sign, which is probably why I relate so strongly to its energy. The main theme of this energy is to find out what makes you unique so you can share it with the world. This energy is associated with the Eleventh House of friendship, so you may find yourself joining groups to help you find a sense of self. If you feel stuck in a rut, call on this energy to help you change your routine or break old habits that no longer serve you. Remember, you have to be a little rebellious and spontaneous to find yourself and influence people.

The futuristic Aquarius new moon encourages you to cut your ties to the past, or at least some of the things that you're still hung up on, and plant seeds of innovation. Aquarius energy is detached, so it can help you make a clean break and boldly start anew. When the new moon is in Aquarius, you're inspired to think outside of the box. Your innovative spirit is off the charts with the new moon in unconventional Aquarius! You may receive flashes of insight during this new moon. This influence allows you to think beyond your emotions and feelings to favor an objective, detached point of view. This is an excellent time to learn new things and brainstorm ideas. Its motto is "I know." Use it to seek innovation, be original, and break existing paradigms. Pay special attention to the ideas that flow through you during this time and manifest what you can. Working on your sacral and solar-plexus chakras is a good idea when working with this energy to wake up your creativity and your powerhouse.

This full moon occurs when the cooperative Aquarius moon opposes the individualistic Leo Sun. This energy helps you see the difference between satisfying the self, as opposed to collaborating with others for the greater good. Also, this energy helps you realize the importance of bringing your "me" energy into group collaborations. That's where great ideas come from! The community-conscious Aquarius full moon reminds you that you are part of something larger than yourself, and that acting on your ideas and ideals will benefit everyone. You may want to go up against an oppressive force or system that gets in your way. This influence brings out the rebel in you, and it can lead to some strange choices if you don't stay grounded. An unbalanced energy comes across as argumentative, stubborn, closed-minded, and dictatorial. It's important to connect to earth energy during a full moon in Aquarius to anchor your energy.

Pisces

Pisces is a mutable water sign ruled by Neptune, whose domain of dreams and delusions works with (or against) Pisces' intuitive, empathetic, and imaginative energy. When you transit through this energy, you can feel a little whimsical, as its dreamy quality encourages heightened imagination and creativity. It is associated with the Twelfth House of the unconscious where your wildest fantasies occur, including versions of yourself that you wish to be. With this energy you don't feel pressured by the series of events in your day planner, and you don't bother checking your watch, because time doesn't exist. Pisces is also about being in an emotional overdrive, where you are more sensitive and receptive to your environment. This energy can often bring confusing experiences to light because it opens you up to deep insight.

A new moon in Pisces inspires you to imagine the future you want, so plant seeds of hope. You'll want to make a list of your biggest dreams, and also a list of what's preventing you from going after them. This energy helps you overcome your fears so you can manifest all that you desire. Its energy is an influence that feels enchanting and full of possibilities, making it an excellent time for manifestation. While Pisces is an emotional sign, when it connects with the energy of the new moon, it allows you to express yourself and your feelings with ease, so this can be a period of profound healing. If you've been wounded emotionally or spiritually, use this sympathetic energy to focus on your regrets, your anger, your insecurities, and your doubts to overcome them. Meditation and creative self-expression are favored during this time.

Pisces is ruled by sensitive, empathetic Neptune, increasing your compassion during this full moon. When the empathy of the Pisces moon combines with the skills of the opposing Virgo Sun, you truly have the best of both worlds. Both signs are service focused, but this energy combination reminds you that you don't have to be precise to be helpful. Perfection is an energetic leak, so if this describes you, use this energy to let lose some of the details. This energy can turn your simple thoughts into vivid fantasies. The tug of war is between idealism and reality. It may seem as though you are being forced to choose a side, but the point of this lunation is to put ideals and inspiration into concrete forms so you can bring your dreams down to earth. There is a mystical energy to this transit that draws you towards spiritual and magical practices, like astrology and tarot reading. Pay attention to your intuition during the full moon in Pisces. When you don't balance these energies during a Pisces full moon, worry, negativity, lack of confidence, seclusion, procrastination, and even sorrow can overtake you.

Sister Zodiac Relationships

In learning about polarity, you know that zodiacs have signs that are the exact opposite on the zodiac wheel, which give us full moons. Because these signs are polar opposites, it is easy to pick up on friction or challenging energy. But, these signs are also perfect pairs in the way they work so well together! Sister signs share their experience twice a year as either a new or full moon. Their opposition exists because where they use their energy (i.e., houses) and different ruling planets help provide alternative views that are intended to challenge you to grow. There exists a love/hate relationship because their elements complement each other, which sustains their inherent connection, and they share the same modality, which creates conflict. When you understand the correlations in their relationships, you can handle any full moon with confidence. Each pairing exists in perfect balance, and they work exceptionally well together.

When the new and full moons come around, you can use their energy to balance yourself with whatever aspect or quality of these parings that you personally lack.

- Aries – Libra: The energy of these cardinal zodiacs wants to create, and boy do they dream big! These signs can build an empire together; their energy can help you build a life you love. Both signs pertain to an active element. Aries is fire, and Libra is air, and when paired, they can help ignite your passion for living and creating. Aries is in the First House of "me" energy, and Libra is in the Seventh House of "we" energy. What may seem like an obstruction along your journey is just figuring out how you can exist authentically in society. Sometimes you need to fight for what you believe in (Aries energy), while other times you need to know when to kill them with kindness (Libra energy). It's a power struggle, but you can navigate it and pick up on the intended messages for you.

- Taurus – Scorpio: The energy of these fixed signs helps you to take a stand for what you started to create or heal under an Aries or Libra moon. The steady energy of these signs refuses to back down. Use this energy to create strong relationships that will help you with whatever you are working toward in your life. Taurus energy is carefree, calm, and grounded, while Scorpio energy works deeply in your emotions and passions. These energies are different, for sure, but they agree that life is worth living to the fullest. The thing to look out for in yourself when working with these energies is your own stubbornness that may be holding you back from creating and living your best life.

- Gemini – Sagittarius: The energy of these mutable signs is hungry for growth through gaining knowledge and information and sharing eye-opening experiences. These energies encourage you to embark on adventures. They emerge after you start to create something big and stand up for yourself in ways that may have been challenging, because these energies need to live freely and have fun as a necessary part of life. These energies are like stress relievers. Also, this energy really helps you to work on inner child issues that you may have. If you six-year-old self wants to swing at a playground, then do it!

- Cancer – Capricorn: The energy of these cardinal signs will make a mark on your life, and possibly help you leave your mark on the world! The balancing act between these two energies relates to home and work life. These energies not only *can* work together, but they *must* also do so. Your home life is about your personal energy ("me" energy), and your work life is about showing up authentically. There are similar energies within the Aries/Libra polarity because they are both cardinal signs, but they are different from an emotional aspect. Cancer energy craves self-care while Capricorn energy takes a tough-love approach. When these energies appear in lunar form, you may feel more stressed or have a hard time handling stress. Don't think for a second that any tension you may experience is caused by your actions under Gemini and Sagittarius energy, as that time of play was necessary. With this energy, you need to decide if you need to indulge in a self-love practice or if you need to kick yourself in the butt and get moving. This doesn't mean the adventure from the preceding sign is over, but while you are creating a life you love, keep watch out for your personal needs and do not forsake your wellness for anything.

- Leo – Aquarius: The energy of these fixed zodiac signs will challenge the status quo but with different approaches, albeit both will be stubborn. These energies are about building strong bonds, but they connect on different levels. Leo is loud and proud and prefers physical touch, while Aquarius, who appears stoic, prefers to engage intellectually and emotionally. While the other fixed signs (Taurus and Scorpio) are about standing up for yourself, these stubborn energies are about authenticity, as well as the collective energy. This energy asks you if you should work on yourself so you can better show up for your humanitarian project or if you should speak out loudly against injustice. If you struggle with this lunar line-up, it's about balancing introverted or withdrawn aspects with extroverted or unrestrained energies to help more than just yourself.

- Virgo – Pisces: These mutable energies of the zodiac help balance reality with idealism, intuition with logic, organization with clutter, and dreams with rational thought. Although these energies seem infinitely different, they are qualities of an empath who ultimately aims to use strengths to help others. This energy will help you find your way in the midst of your personal chaos, or perhaps you are too much in your head and need to listen more to your heart center so you can learn to trust yourself. Because of fears and false limiting beliefs, this energy can be complicated and paralyzing. Use this energy to learn to make the first move toward your best life while learning to trust yourself and what's best for you.

4

PLANETS AND HOUSES

Planetary Energy

I n astrology, the planetary bodies in our solar system each have a "personality"—a symbolic meaning and agency behind their energy. As they travel through the sky, passing through the twelve signs of the zodiac, their personalities come through in various ways. In astrology, things like the Sun, which is actually a star, and the moon, which orbits the Earth, are considered planets. This is also true in the case of Pluto, the dwarf planet; despite its size, it holds as much spiritual significance as all other planets. Planets are important for two reasons, the first being their position at the time of your birth reveals significant information about how you see the world, your habits and traits, belief systems, as well as strengths and weaknesses. Also, as planets move in orbit, they help you understand day-to-day life. And, much like the way you shift your focus during different phases of a lunar cycle, as planets shift in the sky, they also shift your focus in different ways. Here is a simplistic meaning of each planet:

- The Sun – Self-awareness and ego
- The Moon – Inner emotional life
- Mercury – Thinking, timing, and communication
- Mars – Energy and passion
- Venus – Love, beauty, and money
- Saturn – Karma, responsibility, and work
- Jupiter – Spirituality and expansion
- Uranus – Rebellion, individuality, and revolution
- Neptune – Illusion, dreams, and intuition
- Pluto – Power, destruction, and transformation

Planet Retrograde

It's important to note that the Sun, the moon, and the Earth do not retrograde, because only planets that orbit or rotate around the Earth can appear to go in a backward motion. The Sun and Moon do not orbit the Earth. Rather, the Earth orbits the Sun, and the moon rotates around the Earth, but not with the Earth as it rotates around the Sun.[4] When planets in our solar system retrograde (or appear to spin backwards), you'll likely hear people blaming them for the negative circumstances in their lives. Retrograde describes an apparent backwards movement of a planet, but it's only an illusion. More optimistically, the energy of any planetary retrograde is a time for growth. The concept of retrograde can make you feel sluggish here on Earth, but it can also bring about positive changes in your life. Any planet that retrogrades creates a period in time for "re-" words, like refine, reassess, realign, reconnect, refocus, or rethink. The "re-" word you choose should be based on the planets' meanings, solar and lunar energy, and your current personal experience. Here are some examples:

---

[4] NASA, "Earth's Moon – Our Natural Satellite," https://solarsystem.nasa.gov/moons/earths-moon/in-depth/.

- Mercury – Reassess the way you communicate to discover how you can improve.
- Mars – Realign with your goals to make sure you are reaching for your goals, rather than creating "busy" work and achieving nothing.
- Venus – Reevaluate your past relationships to make sure you are living your truth and showing up in relationships authentically.
- Saturn – Reflect on how you previously set boundaries, rethink, and rework them, and consider how you can best communicate them going forward.
- Jupiter – Review your past negative behavior so it won't be repeated.
- Uranus – Real… Get real with yourself, purposely reencounter your fears, and reassess things that aren't working.
- Neptune – Rethink your fantasies and dreams to see if you can turn them into reality.
- Pluto – Refocus on the feelings and ideas you may have been ignoring to help you evolve.

Planetary energies are the building blocks of your astrological identity. They are in constant motion; none of them are stationary. There are a multitude of cosmic combinations that make you unique. An emphasis or lack of emphasis of planets in your personal chart will determine how you are hard-wired. Planets represent the core energies you manifest, and zodiac signs represent how your core energy expresses itself, and finally, houses tell you where the experience will manifest.

Astrological Houses

First, let's differentiate between a zodiac wheel and the wheel of houses. The zodiac wheel is based on the Sun's yearly rotation around Earth and holds unique energetic qualities. The wheel of houses is based on Earth's 24-hour rotation on its own axis,[5] but it is not an energy you can harness. Two people may both have a Libra Sun sign, but one person may have the Libra Sun in the Twelfth House, while the other person may have their Libra Sun in the First House. These distinctions could create two vastly different types of people. The twelve houses of astrology are symbolic of the all the components that make up human life and human experiences. The planets and zodiac signs will manifest most strongly in the sphere of life represented by the house in which they fall on your birth chart. Houses have no energetic quality, like elements or planets, and they do not express energy as a zodiac sign does. The houses are simply a location indicating where these energies discussed in this book manifest.

A house is an area of expertise, or a file of experience, rather than the actual experience. Houses are in order following the developmental path of human life, from the original impulse of individual being (the First House of self), to learning what is yours and how to use the material objects you own (the Second House of money and possessions), to learning how to communicate within your environment (the Third House of communication), and so on. The most important houses (house one, four, seven, and ten) are angular, because the cusps coincide with four special angles on a birth chart and planets in these houses will influence you the most: ascendant, descendant, the Midheaven (MC), and the Lower Heaven (IC). These are like your personal compass points that orient you to the cosmos. Any planet on the MC is facing due south, and any planet on your IC is facing due north.

Every part of your birth chart shows something about you and your life, and each position rules something different. The three aspects of your Primal Triad—your Sun sign (your inner self), your moon sign (your emotional self), and your

---

[5] Astrology Library, "12 Astrological Houses – Astrology Lesson 4," https://astrolibrary.org/.

ascendant or rising sign (your outer self) form the basis of who you are as a person. This is reminiscent of the "as above," "so below," also "flows within" concept from Chapter One. Your ascendant indicates the sign that was rising on the eastern horizon at the time and location of your birth. The qualities of this energy permeate your being and therefore, are how you outwardly project your energy to the world. It's that first and lasting impression you make on the world. Remember how we discussed polarities earlier in this book? Well, your descendant sign is the opposite side of the zodiac from your ascendant sign, meaning it lies on an axis of opposing zodiac signs. So, while your ascendant describes how the world sees you, your descendant describes how you see the world. It's the relationship between "we" and "me" with your own personal energy.

The ascendant and descendant make up your horizontal axis, the IC and MC make up your vertical axis, or top and bottom of your chart. It divides your East energy from your West energy. It shows where you come from and where your soul wants to go in this lifetime. IC is the acronym for the Latin phrase *Imum Coeli*, meaning "bottom of the sky."[6] This point on your chart provides information about the depths of your soul and clarifies your authentic self. Your soul came to Earth for a specific purpose, but while here you have certain things that influence who you become. The private self, what you hold inside and rarely show people, is made up of habits and thought patterns created from early childhood experiences. MC is the acronym for the Latin term *Medium Coeli*, meaning "top of the sky."[7] This point represents your life path and how to outwardly express your authenticity and live true to your purpose. This is what people can see, such as your material accomplishments. So, your IC is your emotional inner child, and your MC rectifies your

---

[6] Katie Robertson, "What's 'IC' in the Birth Chart?" https://www.astrology.com/article/ic-astrology/.

[7] *Ibid.*

inner energy into a socially acceptable package. If you live your life based on false and limiting beliefs, then you will never reach your soul's purpose. Wild Moon Healing attempts to rectify that. But, the topic right now isn't healing, it's houses, so let's examine each house more closely.

First House

The first astrological house is the house of self or personality, and it's ruled by Aries and the planet Mars. The cusp of the First House is the home of the ascendant, the sign that was rising on the eastern horizon at the precise moment of one's birth. By thinking of this in terms of sunrise and new beginnings, one begins to grasp the concepts of the First House. Embark on new beginnings of finding self and the realization of your own potential. This includes self-awareness, the physical body, personality, and appearance. It also represents your personal views on life, self-identity, self-image, early childhood environment, and beginnings. This house provides clues as to how you initiate newness, and how you may be impulsive. Any planets in this house will greatly influence your personality and how others perceive you. Beginning the process of evolving into a unique individual is one of the greatest contributions you can make to the world.

Second House

The Second House refers to your own money and possessions, what you value, your hidden talents, sense of self-worth, and self-esteem. It's about how you value yourself, instead of describing your personality as in the First House. Possessions include anything a person owns (except the house/home, which is ruled by the Fourth House): cars, furniture, clothing, moveable property, investments, and securities. The Second House specifies how you earn and spend your own money (as opposed to other people's money in the Eighth House), your attitude towards wealth and material possessions, and your potential for accumulating wealth. To a great extent, your possessions, why you have them, and what you do with them help to define your character. Within this house, personal freedom is established by your financial capability and sensibility. While this speaks to that which you own, it's not limited simply to tangible things. You own your feelings and emotions, as well as your inner self, abilities, needs, and wants. When you own up to anything, you are in fact claiming ownership of your greatest possession: yourself.

Third House

The Third House is that of communication, which by extension includes one's immediate environment: siblings, neighbors, short journeys, and all forms of transportation. In this house, much of the communication is going on between you and those you hold close. While communication can come in both written and verbal forms, it also has a conscious quality to it to help you listen. The Third House also includes the intellect, the lower mind (details and small bits of information as opposed to the higher mind of consciousness in the Ninth House), thinking patterns, early education (before college), analytical ability, and a basic grasp of things, and a practical sensibility. Communication includes messages, deliveries, gossip, phone calls, visits, reading, and writing—some of which can be energetic leaks. In dealing with the concrete knowledge you possess, watch out for ruthless ambition and greed. Harnessing your intelligence and sharing it effectively with others is the essence of the Third House.

Fourth House

The Fourth House refers to the home and everything associated with it, including your upbringing. It is about your foundation and roots—the very ground where you were born and raised. See how the cusp of the Fourth House is the IC, the lowest point on the chart, and representative of things "as below." The Fourth House can provide clues to your karmic lesson for this lifetime and reveals the karmic baggage you brought with you into this life. Even if you don't believe in reincarnation, you're likely to be surprised by what you find in your Fourth House—it may move your soul. Any planets in the Fourth House affect your home life, your emotions, your subconscious, and possibly your relationship with your parents. The Fourth House brings things full circle by also addressing old age, endings, and your final resting place—starting with the earth you were born on and ending there as well. This house is about tangible property but also the home inside of you. You work hard to create a safe sanctuary to come home to, but it is also about what refuge you can provide your inner self. The sentiment of "I'm home" doesn't refer to just a physical space, because when you feel safe inside, you are always home. The Fourth House represents family, history, and traditions, all of which contribute to the process of becoming a true, actualized, and individualized self. This is how you come home.

Fifth House

The Fifth House refers to creativity and the pursuit of pleasure. Oftentimes pleasure is the result of creating something to share with the world, but it also refers to the procreation of children. This house includes personal interests, love affairs, sports, hobbies, speculation, risk-taking, teaching, drama, and creative self-expression. The Fifth House is all about you being yourself and enjoying it! Interestingly, romance, dating, love affairs, and sexual relationships are ruled by this Fifth House, yet marriage is assigned to the seventh. Why? Because the old energy of marriage was not entered into for pleasure. Marriage was arranged or entered into as a contract to procreate and raise kids to preserve family values and culture. Since the new energy of marriage is to marry for love, just remember that affairs of the heart are in the Fifth House, but cooperative partnerships are in the domain of the Seventh House. The Fifth House encourages a creative life, one from which you can derive much personal enjoyment and self-satisfaction, so play for the purpose of emotional enrichment and pure pleasure. We are all creative beings.

Sixth House

The Sixth House is commonly referred to as the house of health. It refers to daily work, service, diet, health, illness, and your physical ability to work. This house really involves the quality of your work and the quality of the jobs you perform, as opposed to an actual career (career is represented by the Tenth House). This house includes the daily mundane tasks, including personal hygiene and your method of reacting or responding to everyday crises, illnesses, and reversals of fortune. Basically, how you confront adversity and deal with the lessons they invariably teach helps to define the person you become. A sense of duty, responsibility, and personal growth all contribute to the creation of an achieved being. Don't let your sense of service cause you to neglect your self-care. The simplistic tasks of a day, starting with what you will wear to humanitarian efforts, whether you perform them in good health or not, help to create a fulfilling life.

Seventh House

The Seventh House is referred to as the house of partnerships. It is sometimes referred to as the house of marriage, but it encompasses all one-to-one relationships: marriage, business partnerships, contracts, and cooperative relationships. Just as with the chakra system, where the first three of the main chakras are environment and the top three are internal, the focus on this house shifts away from self and focuses on others. Relationships governed by this house are contractually and permanently binding relationships. How you cooperate and share in the relationship and how the relationship serves some functional purpose in the larger social community is also governed here. Planets in this house will influence your manner of relating to others. They also give clues to issues that may arise in your relationships. Having a purpose that results in the act of accomplishing something for the greater good is particularly important to this house. Tension in partnerships should be viewed as lessons, so this house also has a dark side, including things such as divorce, separation, quarrels, open enemies, and lawsuits. How you react to this adversity helps to shape partnerships or create enemies that can cause or stop war.

Eighth House

Simply put, the Eighth is the polar opposite of the Second House. Where the Second rules your own individual possessions, the Eighth House rules what a relationship owns (joint finances). This house governs death, regeneration, taxes, inheritances, wills, legacies, sex (the actual act of sex), latent occult ability, joint resources, your partner's/spouse's money and possessions, bankruptcy, losses, personal sacrifices, alimony, and clairvoyance. The emphasis on sex is how an orgasm results in leaving a piece of itself behind. In this life you will experience death and rebirth many times, through failed relationships leading to new ones or career changes, for example. You regenerate and become reborn with each new phase, should you allow it. This house is often misunderstood, because the things represented here appear to have nothing in common and tend toward the negative. But this house is about transformative powers and healing. Transformation requires some type of death, loss, surrender, or even injury to invoke change. This house rules those processes and things by which you transform and become more authentic. This house begs the question, "What legacy will you leave behind?"

Ninth House

The Ninth House refers to philosophy, religion, law, learning, higher education (as opposed to early education in the Third House), ethics, morals, long journeys, travel, foreign countries and interests, spiritual urges, dreams, visions, higher mind, ideas, understanding, wisdom, books, publishing, ceremonies, and rituals. This is the house of big thoughts and big ideas—moreover, it's about a voyage of discovery to search for personal meaning in this life. The concept of this house is understanding, but on a more complex level than the Third House, which rules knowledge. Understanding involves the synthesis of known data. The Third and Ninth Houses symbolize the two polarities of the human mind, the concrete and the abstract. The unknown is understood through your spiritual journey, accepting that which is greater than you. The Ninth House also includes experiences that you encounter when you search for a deeper meaning of things. Whatever expands your field of activity or the scope of your mind—long journeys, direct contact with other cultures, vivid dreams, and even Moon work and working with the energies described in this book. It all boils down to understanding what you see and feel, and then probing further in hopes of realizing its true meaning (i.e., the essence of Moon work).

Tenth House

The Tenth House is the house of social status, honor, community power, prestige, reputation, and professional career. In our society, this includes financial success but only as it relates to community, power, prestige, and the authority that comes with it. It's not about gaining "material stuff," as it is in the Second House. The desire of the Tenth House is success for the sake of honor and social status. This house includes social foundations (as opposed to personal foundations of the Fourth House), recognition, personal achievements, promotions, social responsibilities, sense of duty, and authority figures. This house encompasses the most public areas of one's life and the career that you grow into—as opposed to daily work and odd jobs ruled by the Sixth House. There is a parental energy in this house, like in the Fourth House, but this energy is more about who wears the pants and has the most authority. As with the other angular houses, any planets in this house are especially important. Planets in the Tenth House, the sign on the cusp of the Tenth House, and its ruling planet will greatly influence your career and your general reputation in public. Ultimately, will your ego manage your power and authority to truly help society, or will your energy be more willful and reckless? How you treat others is an especially important personal characteristic to evaluate.

Eleventh House

The Eleventh House is the house of friendships, community, large groups, and friends. It refers to memberships, hopes, goals, ambitions, wishes, social groups, networking, professional associations, and humanitarian interests. It is through your friends and group activities that you add substance and meaning to your life and to society. Also, it refers to self-realization, liberty, legislation, and regulation. It is about strength in numbers—the power in the collective "we" energy. As you interact with groups in your environment, focus on what you bring to the table and how you make a difference. Don't take on too much, as that is an energetic leak. Evaluate your actions that you do by virtue of the collective. Work to remain authentic and true to yourself and your destiny. The group can expand your desires, hopes, and dreams that you want to realize—the power of collective creation. Together "we" can create so much more than one can alone. It is always best to bring your true self to the group, so by nature of diversity, you can go beyond your own thinking.

Twelfth House

The Twelfth House refers to the subconscious, the hidden self that exists apart from our physical everyday reality. This is the house of the unseen realm, sorrow, shadows, and of invisible enemies, including the unconscious mind (you could be your own worst enemy), subconscious memory, subconscious habit patterns from the past (neuroplasticity), mental illness, karmic debts, self-deception, escapism, spiritual realization, limitations, frustration, and ultimately our self-undoing. The unconscious state can help you stimulate your successes and cope with your failures. On a physical, material level, the Twelfth House includes things that take us away from everyday life: institutions (i.e., hospitals, prisons, and government offices), places of confinement, secrets, secret relationships, and self-sacrifice for others. It also refers to tribulations, widowhood, grief, funerals, exile, seclusion, bribery, subversion, murder, suicide, kidnapping, and endings. For those who believe, the Twelfth House is also considered to refer to the collective unconscious of all humanity. This house might more aptly be called the House of Reckoning, since it is here that you review what you've done and how you've been, then decide where to go from there. This house speaks to your shadows and the act of conducting shadow work, dealing with repressed memories, trauma, and secrets, and the manner in which you will be reborn or transformed. Sounds like another good name for his house is the House of Despair, but it is ultimately a champion of positive transformation to better equip you to move forward. Remember, when doing shadow work, you have all the answers you need inside of you. By visiting this house, you will gain insight into what the future will bring you.

Houses of the Planets and Signs

Each planet and zodiac sign is naturally associated with a house—the house that most corresponds to its archetype. The planet, then, is said to be the *natural ruler* of that house, or more often, it's said to be *at home* in that house. The qualities of the zodiac signs are not exactly the same as those of the houses with which they are associated. There are subtle differences between the energies of each of the signs and houses.

- The First House of self, life, and body is found in Aries and ruled by Mars.
- The Second House of possessions and money is found in Taurus and ruled by Venus.
- The Third House of communication and short journeys is found in Gemini and ruled by Mercury.
- The Fourth House of home, family, and roots is found in Cancer and ruled by the moon.
- The Fifth House of creativity, children, and fun is found in Leo and ruled by the Sun.
- The Sixth House of health, service, work, and routine is found in Virgo and ruled by Mercury.
- The Seventh House of contractual relationships is found in Libra and ruled by Venus.

- The Eighth House of sex, death, and inheritance is found in Scorpio, naturally ruled by Pluto, and traditionally ruled by Mars.
- The Ninth House of travel, higher education, and spirituality is found in Sagittarius and ruled by Jupiter.
- The Tenth House of career, social position, and dominant yin/yang energy is found in Capricorn and ruled by Saturn.
- The Eleventh House of friendships, associations, and aspirations is found in Aquarius and naturally ruled by Uranus, traditionally ruled by Saturn.
- The Twelfth House of the unconscious, clandestine relationships, and secret enemies is found in Pisces, naturally ruled by Neptune, and traditionally ruled by Jupiter.

Spiritual Direction

You discovered when reading about astrological houses that the ascendant, descendant, the Midheaven (MC), and the Lower Heaven (IC) in your birth chart create a personal compass rose, thereby invoking spirituality in the directions. No matter how long you've traveled in the wrong direction, you can always turn around and create your sacred space to call in healing or change. The spiritual journey is often a lonely path, especially during difficult or trying times, when you are changing your life and using all of your energy to not fall back into old negative behavioral patterns. There is a sacred circle of direction, known as the Medicine Wheel in some traditions or as the Sacred Space in others. Honoring the directions of this space is a widespread spiritual practice in ancient and contemporary nature wisdom traditions, which you can implement to create and connect with sacred space. Spiritual direction is energy in motion, and each direction has energy of its own. The four cardinal directions are north, south, east, and west. To add three-dimensional space, there is also up and down, or "as above, so below." Some add a central point. I use it to represent my personal harmony and agreement with nature, my inner-self, and the spark of passion that resides inside. Remember, everything you do in your spiritual practice is personal. You should feel free to adapt whatever practices you want and alter them to fit your own needs. The descriptions below provide a framework for working with directions.

Up represents the direction of the sky and cosmos. In nature it's the Sun, moon, planets, stars, meteors, galaxies, and deep space. This direction in your life represents your consciousness or higher self, but also liberation and vision. Up is also spiritual—angelic beings, universe, God, and Source. As you contemplate all that is above, see yourself there and reflect on creation legends or the science of evolution to discover your truth.

Down speaks of the earth, grounding, nature, and the realm of death/transformation. It also represents the biosphere of the planet and all that lives there. In reflecting with this direction, contemplate what your energetic imprint will be on Earth. What will your legacy entail? Visualize yourself as part of the tapestry of life and how you commune with all living things, including nature as well as other people in your community and beyond.

East, the direction of the rising Sun, represents new beginnings, fresh vision, rebirth, and ascension. It is represented by the insightful element of air and the spring season, when the earth awakens and brings beauty back to the land. This time of year is the time of the new moon, where you awaken recharged, ready to begin new adventures—think about the power of your mind and your ability to map out the life you want, and then create it. In the thinking realm, take note of your thought process, reasoning, attitude, and your mental health. From a healing perspective, examine your self-talk, practice positive affirmations, and write in your journal to get your thoughts onto paper. If you think you can, you will; if you think you cannot, you won't. Likewise, if you look for things to make you smile, you will find them; if you focus on things that upset you, you will find those as well. Also, think about how you can grow through education and experiential learning.

South is about creation, sparked by the element of fire and the beginning of the summer season. The element fire is expressed through lightning, campfires, and fireflies that light up under the safety of the moon. With the Sun high in the sky, your inner child comes alive and becomes curious. Life engages here. This time of year is the time of the waxing lunar cycle where you want to execute inspired, meaningful action to help you on your new adventures—think about the power of action and your ability to take action to create a life you love. Examine how you spend your time and if you are using your time wisely. Balance your time to appropriately allot for work, play, and alone time. Identify any destructive behavior patterns or habits and focus on positive behavioral changes. In looking at time management, make sure play and exercise are included in your schedule. Set small manageable goals and achieve them!

The direction west is about transformation. It is represented by the cleansing element of water and the fall season ushering in a time of change. Water is all around and inside us, from oceans, streams, dew, rain, and fluids in your own body—including the tears you cry. This time of year is the time of the full moon, where you start energy work to release old habits, pains, or patterns that hold you back—think about how the power of your emotions can transform your life. The emotional realm is hard because it requires vulnerability. Pay attention to your moods and feelings toward yourself and others. In relationships consider your level of intimacy (not sex) and trust. Practice guided imagery/visualizations, active listening, expressing and sharing your feelings, or giving and receiving comfort. If you have trouble expressing your emotions with words, look to artistic and creative expressions such as dance, drawing, or even cooking.

North is like a guiding light, much like that of the North Star. It is represented by the grounding element of earth and seen in nature as rocks and soil. North is represented by the hour of midnight, within the cycle of a day where the veil between worlds grows thin, and the season of winter. This time of year is the time of the waning lunar cycle that supports going inward to comprehend the deeper mysteries of your healing journey. This direction is about the energy of insightful discovery of the physical—think about the power of your body and your ability to take care of your physical body. Pay attention to your physical body and its messages through sensations. Healing modalities include good nutrition, physical exercise, hygiene, and body language. Remember your body needs rest and relaxation to perform optimally.

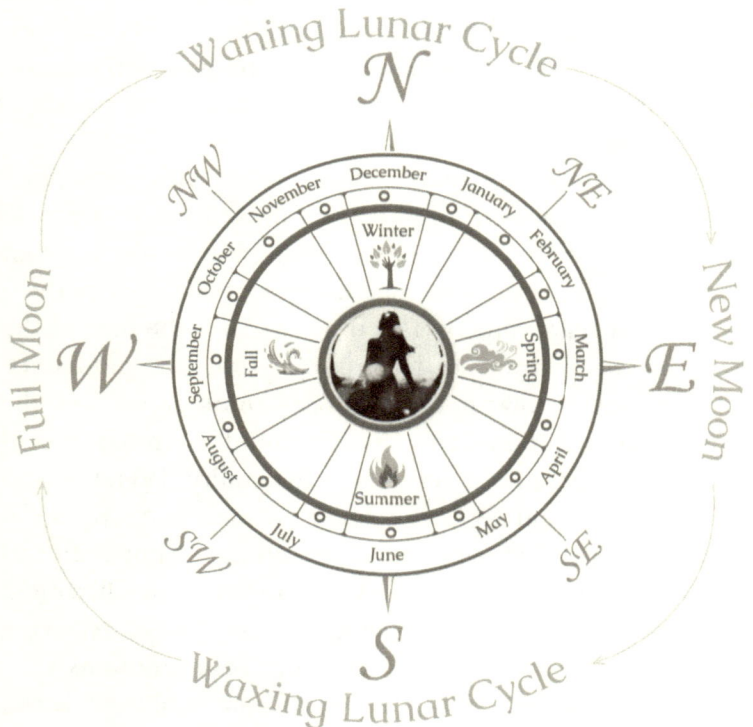

Directional Invocation

In performing an invocation and to really enforce the energy you are trying to create, mark or identify the directions in your space so you can face the appropriate way when reciting this invocation. Center yourself with your crossed hands held to your heart. As you speak to each direction, raise your hands and call in its energy, or outstretch your hands and pull its energy in toward your heart. Always end each direction by thanking the energy or any guides that show up for you. Begin from the North, representing your physical body, raise or stretch out your hands, and speak to it or recite something such as the passage below. As with all spiritual practices, work to make this unique to who you are and your needs. For example, turn this practice into a ritual dance to express your honor. Create the habit of journaling afterwards to note your experience or revelations that occurred to ultimately help you establish an understanding of this energy and its association to helping you find your truth. Live authentically and create a life you love.

Invocation

From the North, I call in the long nights where I spend more time resting, to attune to my body and its needs, as well as commune with my ancestors to help ripen my wisdom and guide me on my journey. *(Give thanks.)*

From the East, I call in the rising Sun to awaken me. As easily as the eagle glides in the air, I attune to my mind and gain insight on what I want to create to bring beauty back into my life. *(Give thanks.)*

From the South, I call in the summer heat to ignite in me a passion so deep that I may fully engage in life, finding inspiration and meaning everywhere I look. *(Give thanks.)*

From the West, I call in the fully illuminated moon to cast light on what I need to change and provide clarity on that which is holding me back from my full potential as I attune to my feelings. *(Give thanks.)*

From Above, I call in energy from my Source to help me sink into faith, where I know my Source will never leave me, forget me, or overlook me. (Look up and experience yourself connecting to Source). *(Give thanks.)*

From Below, I call in energy from the earth to ground me and raise my vibration to a prosperous level to share with all living things. (Bend over and touch the ground. Visualize yourself connecting to the web of life.) *(Give thanks.)*

May all of this energy flowing within me shine as love through my heart center so I leave a positive energetic imprint in this world. Thank you.

5

THE ENERGY OF NUMBERS

Numerology

Numerology is a system of vibrations and an aspect of astrology that can help with self-discovery, intuitive predictions, and unmanifested potential. It studies the mystical energetic relationship between numbers, letters, and patterns. Perhaps the first numbers were represented as scratch marks in stone, possibly tracking the phases of the moon, giving us a glimpse of the innermost workings of the human mind. Way back in ancient Babylonia, the Chaldeans observed the movement of planets and recorded them as numbers to predict cosmic phenomena such as eclipses.[8] We in modern civilization are still in awe of the Egyptian pyramids, which certainly required numbers and calculations. We've all heard

---

[8] Martin Shuttleworth, "Mesopotamian Astronomy," https://explorable.com/mesopotamian-astronomy.

about Greek mythology, but the followers of Pythagoreanism, a cult in ancient Greece, believed that the universe and all that is above work together in numeric harmony. They believed in the cosmic significance of "fourness," which implies 1 + 2 + 3 + 4 = 10, which is a perfect triangle.[9] (Remember those pyramids!)

They believed the way these numbers fit together created order. They even taught opposites, and thus balance, in the form of even and odd numbers. Aristotle referred to the "table of ten opposites" as limit/unlimited, odd/even, one/many, right/left, male/female, rest/motion, straight/curved, light/darkness, good/evil, and square/oblong.[10] This was the origin of thoughts about duality that we see all throughout the study of metaphysics—to everything there is an opposite that creates energetic balance.

Numerology is a tool that can help you gain a greater understanding of who you are, who others are around you, and how everything is connected. Numbers can help you find the concealed meaning of life—your life based on energetic strengths and weaknesses, based on the numbers in your birth date and the letters in your given name (see exercises in Chapter Nine).

---

[9] Ian Stewart, "Number Symbolism," https://www.britannica.com/topic/number-symbolism.

[10] Holger Thesleff, "Pythagoreanism," https://www.britannica.com/science/Pythagoreanism.

Nikola Tesla had a strong understanding of the relationship between numbers and the universe. He said, "If you only knew the magnificence of the 3, 6, and 9, then you would have a key to the universe."[11] He also stated, "If you want to find the secrets of the universe, think in terms of energy, frequency, and vibration."[12] Just like everything else discussed in this book, numbers have a vibrational energetic frequency and pattern that help make up the human experience. You welcomed the world with your soul's presence at an exact time and in a precise place, and that was by divine purpose. Isn't it great to know that you started living your life on purpose and that you always have a divine purpose for being here? The energy of numbers is imprinted in you for your lifetime, making it an appropriate companion to astrology. Numbers can clarify your astrology chart by providing additional knowledge to help enhance your understanding of yourself. By studying numerology, you could find some superpower you are divinely gifted that you haven't unlocked yet.

The exercises toward the end of the book help you calculate numbers to learn more about who you are. The digital root is a mathematical calculation that deduces a number to the smallest possible number by adding all the numbers together. For example, the date of June 23, 2023, would be calculated as $6 + 2 + 3 + 2 + 2 + 3 = 18 = 1 + 8 = 9$. This day should have a healing quality to it, as is one of the qualities of the number nine. There are many calculations using the numbers in your date of birth, or using the letters in your name, to provide you with more information about yourself.

- Your life path number influences your entire being because it tells you who you are at your core, and who you are learning to be, so you can live authentically toward your life's purpose.

---

[11] Kaleena Fraga. "Inside Nikola Tesla's 3, 6, 9 Obsession And The Unusual Theories It Spawned," https://allthatsinteresting.com/nikola-tesla-3-6-9.

[12] Kristie Pursey, "6 Nikola Tesla Quotes That Might Change the Way You See the World," https://www.learning-mind.com/nikola-tesla-quotes/#google_vignette

- Your birth number provides information about your younger self. For instance, the day of your birth shows how your formative years affect your current experience, and the year of your birth reflects how you interact with other people.
- Your attitude number tells you what you can change to better yourself and move into your authenticity.
- Your destiny number knows where you are going—it reveals information about opportunities that may come your way to help you achieve your life's purpose.
- The soul urge number represents what your heart and soul crave more than anything in this world, and it reveals your motivation and the lens through which you make decisions.

If your life and soul urge numbers are the same, you may notice you have an easy time being you—you are in energetic harmony. If they are different, you may notice there is conflict in your life when trying to live authentically.

By understanding the meanings of these basic numbers in numerology, you can also better understand the profound energetic messages divinely sent to you. It's as if numbers have their own personalities, and like the personalities of the people in your life, the meanings of numbers influence your life in different ways. When you feel lost or stagnant, you can use numbers to help you get back on track. You can find the answers to so many questions in numbers, such as, "Why did I excel at a task and my friend failed miserably?" Numbers can help you make decisions about relationships, health, education, and even finances. Knowing specific numbers based on your birthdate and name can help you set goals and plan to achieve success, as well as help provide you with information to shift out of difficult and complex situations. In numerology the nine single-digit numbers are building blocks. Understanding the basic meaning of each number helps you unlock their hidden message (pay attention to repeating numbers and patterns of numbers that you may see). You can never change your past, but you can create your best life going forward, and numerology is a gateway to that change. Just as your astrology birth chart contains powerful metaphysical insights—the planets and zodiac signs are connected to specific attributes—the teachings of numerology can also offer insights on personality, future events, and even life's greater purpose. Let's start by exploring the energy of each number.

Divinatory Significance

I love numbers and I see numbers in all things. I learned the information in this section on the meaning of the numbers from my mentor, teacher, and good friend, Dr. Gwen MacGregor. She's taught me many things, and I am so grateful for her. Before giving broader meaning to each number, I want to introduce a simple key to interpreting numbers inherited from ancient traditions for the first nine. The following table lays out the typical symbolic correspondences for these numbers.

Number Divinatory Meaning

- One – Initiative, independence, forcefulness (masculine energy number)
- Two – Diplomatic, tact, attention to detail (feminine energy number)
- Three – Spiritual, ambition, self-expression, easy success, lucky
- Four – Material labor, routine work with little monetary compensation, unlucky
- Five – Imagination, inventive genius, charm, restlessness, adventurous
- Six – Tenacity, conscientiousness, success by working with another, domestic

- Seven – Mysticism, magick, occultism, isolation, poets, dreamers, misunderstood
- Eight – Judgment, reason, organization, financial success
- Nine – Sympathy, generosity, dramatic, artistic talent (higher octave – teacher/master)

Do you see a pattern to their symbolism—As Above, So Below? You can divide the first eight numbers into two groups. There is a spiritual group as with the top three chakras and an earthly group as with the bottom three chakras. Then the nine is counterbalancing them all as with the heart chakra. Within numbers there exists vast limitless potential and amazing energy.

The Energy of Numbers

Numbers are as crucial as the alphabet. Numbers play an important role in day-to-day life—in every situation you face. Real life is based on transactional activities, achievements, and downgrades that you can measure. Numbers are the building blocks to feeling confident and secure. The more success you accumulate, the better you feel. You can use numerology to help you discover more truths about who you are. All you need is the date of your birth, and you can unlock the meaning in your birthday and the path you are destined to walk down in this lifetime. For your birthday number, just research the day you were born. If you were born on the 3rd of the month, then your number is three. If you were born on a date with double digits, you need to add them together. For example, if you were born on the 28th day of the month, your calculation would look like this: 2 + 8 = 10. For this one calculation, do not reduce this to a single number, your birthday number would be 10. Someone with a birth number of ten would be energetic, cheerful, and independent.

Each number has strengths, weaknesses, and personality traits associated with it. This level of detail helps you delve deeper into yourself to discover why you do things the way you do and what traits might cause you to get into trouble.

Number One

Number one is a proactive force representing newness in all the possibilities that await you but at its core it reflects the root of opportunity in your life. It is a reflection of your confidence and personal power and seeks to have you examine your current circumstance. The main reason for the universe reflecting number one in your life is to remind you that you have all that you need within you to change your current circumstance, thereby inspiring you to create your future and embrace a new beginning.

Characteristics reflecting strengths of the number one are independence, innovation, and goal orientation—you're a natural born leader with a seemingly endless pool of creative ideas within you. Your authentic self may be more eccentric than others, but that's okay. You must be authentic to fully manifest your innate characteristics. Number ones are confident in their abilities and unafraid to make difficult decisions. These people are very success oriented. The message from seeing a number one repeatedly is that you have the potential to be self-sufficient, positive, and creative. You are likely an innovative mind that can see opportunities that others miss.

Characteristics reflecting the weaknesses of this number are forcefulness, taking unnecessary risk, and being suspicious. When you are vibrating at a lower energy level, you may be overly ambitious, uncaring, domineering, reckless, and you may lack foresight and have tunnel vision. The worst part of low-vibing number-one energy is self-doubt and having a deep fear of making a mistake or falling short of your goal. Of all the numbers, one is by far its own worst critic. The slightest criticism hurts deeply, but you will ultimately use it as motivation to improve your life and focus on your potential rather than your shortcomings. However, you enjoy challenges because it makes victory that much sweeter.

If your life path number is one and you are resonating with a high personal vibration, you are an innovator and pioneer of sorts. You are full of motivation and leadership energy. But, a strong leader requires a loyal following. Your enthusiasm is infectious, and your commitment inspires others to action. You may clash with other number ones, people with big personalities, or with people who don't like being led. You create opportunities for yourself by learning your lessons in all your life experiences, which builds your confidence.

In tarot, the number one card is The Magician, advising you to use all available resources to manifest possibilities and create your future. In the zodiac, the number one is associated with both Aries and Leo energy, as both these astrology signs thrive in activity, freedom, and self-expression.

Your shadow aspects may concern how you believe you are the only qualified person in your group. Don't let overconfidence and arrogance knock you off your game. Sometimes the healthy thing to do is to let go of winning and find balance. Please remember to be kind to yourself and don't let your ego keep you from asking for help when things get rough. You never have to struggle alone.

Number Two

Number two is about relationships and dualities. It is the most intuitive number and could be divinely directing you to be more empathetic. When you have two of anything, a need for balance is created, so this number naturally crafts harmony and teamwork. If you see this number repeat, then the universe is showing you both sides of a situation in an unbiased way. If you unravel the message too late, you may be indecisive or easily hurt.

Compared to number ones, a number two would be the sidekick, as it is completely opposite in personality. The strengths of number two are intuitiveness, influence, and unity—a true diplomat. This number tells you that you are instinctually aware of people's emotions before they even express them. Of course, this intuitive gift should be used for the greatest good—so you can offer support and compassion. You may cry at sad movies and dislike watching the news. You work best when you connect with your powerful intuition. You are tactful and proactive, helping to create balance through cooperation and influence. Two is about duality, so this implies you can see both sides to a situation that requires balance, thus you hate conflict.

When you are vibrating at a lower energy level, you may be indecisive, easily hurt, and unassertive. You may be overly sensitive to outside energies that can throw you off balance by making you feel you need to put your own needs aside. You may quietly struggle, staying in a negative or unpleasant situation for too long because familiar feels safe to you. The worst part of this negative energy is that number twos can get stuck in inaction. If your life path is number two, you have the ability to be quite a powerful influencer, but you do so quietly behind the scenes.

The number two in tarot is quite fitting, The High Priestess, which is the most intuitive of all the tarot cards. This number is associated in the zodiac with Taurus and Cancer energy, because of your silent tenacity and overall pleasant nature.

Your shadows include the parts of you that constantly undervalue your contribution because you compare yourself to others, as most people do, but your sensitive nature can cause you to self-doubt more than others. Work on setting healthy boundaries to protect your energy—you do not need to feel anyone's pain or carry anyone's burdens but your own.

Number Three

Number three is about trinity. Think of groups such as the father, son, and Holy Ghost, or Hecate, the triple goddess of the maiden, mother, and crone. The skill associated with this number is to build your own group of friends, lovers, and kindred spirits through communication. Number three is about originality, such as unique thinking and creative expression that allows you to convey an abstract idea in a way that others will miss when you are not around. If you keep seeing the number three, the universe is probably telling you to have fun and embody all that that means.

The strengths of number three are that you are communicative, artistic, and charming—a natural entertainer. You shine through all forms of expression including art when you can't find the right written or spoken words. Because of your demeanor and communication skills, you are very magnetic without ever trying. You may be known for your sharp wit and exaggerated storytelling ability. You have a certain optimistic energy about you and always see the glass as half full.

When you are vibrating at a lower energy level, you may be naïve, unfocused, and shallow. You may not have mature wisdom, which leads to making poor life decisions, which puts you, and possibly others, in a bad situation. Being full of enthusiastic energy keeps your mind running and your eyes only looking at the superficial things in life, because you don't have much experience going deeper on an emotional level. Your motto may be pleasure before growth. If you have a life path number of three, others may see you as exciting, charming, and upbeat. Taking a journey of personal growth will be beneficial to you.

Then number three card in tarot is The Empress, a card of creativity and fertility. The zodiac energy associated with this number is Gemini and Sagittarius, as both like to live it up and thrive on enjoyable experiences. Learn to express your deep thoughts. If words escape you, then tap into your creative talents. Draw, paint, cook, or dance to show your true expression.

In shadow, you live for an audience and can become depressed without the company of others—learn to control your moods and really strive to enjoy some alone time. Working on self-discipline to battle procrastination will help you through any hard times.

Number Four

Number four lets you know you can rescue yourself through strength and efficiency. If you keep seeing this number, you need to get serious, put your head down, and do the work. Lead with your head, not your heart. See things for what they are: right or wrong, black or white. There is no wiggle room or grey matter. The universe is telling you it is here to support you and can lend a great amount of support if you allow it. Stick to the tried-and-true approach to accomplishing things. Some cultures believe the number four to be unlucky, but it actually shows up when you are having a hard time so divine energy can express support for you.

The strengths of number four are that you are practical, loyal, and service-oriented—a brilliant example of self-discipline. You have a realistic view on life, make wise decisions, and develop solid plans for forward growth. You pride yourself on being dependable and hardworking and use those attributes to create a strong foundation in any relationship. You enjoy putting things together, such as a puzzle or craft project, and take pride in your finished product. To really feel happy, secure, and stable, you need a solid plan, and your detail-oriented self knows how to put things in their proper place. You may be a declutter diva, because your organization skills are the stuff of legends, and your home reflects that—a safe, organized haven.

When you are vibrating at a lower energy level, you may be dogmatic, rigid, and dull. You may be conservative and perfectly content the way you are—never allowing yourself to be swayed. Be careful not to view your personal opinions and false limiting beliefs as fact. A number four personality may have a lot to learn about teamwork. If your life path number is four, you are most likely practical and focused on service and hard work.

The number four card in tarot is The Emperor, who is stoic, responsible, and practical. In the zodiac a number four is associated with Cancer energy, the fourth sign, because it works hard to create a secure environment.

In shadow, others may feel inhibited in the way you approach a situation from a logical, measured, and practical viewpoint, because you view rules as freedom, which some will find unnerving. If you are feeling stuck, it's because you fear taking risks. Sometimes it's really not that much better to be safe than sorry.

Number Five

The energy of number five follows number four so beautifully. You've done the work; now it's time to get out and experiment. It brings a sense of adventure, with no fear about where you will land. If you have been craving excitement and freedom, this energy shows up to help you change. The only thing number five is attached to is being unattached. The universe will help you go with the flow and thrive in your new experiences. If you allow it, you will begin to feel refreshed with high-vibrational energy and full of possibilities.

The strengths of number five are being curious, adaptable, flexible, outgoing, social, and energetic. You are the epitome of a bubbly, free-spirited person because of your charismatic personality. You are open and never short on words. The curious nature of this energy is best spent through experiential learning. This energy is emotionally detached, free, flourishes in social settings, and never misses the chance to learn new things from people different than themselves. If someone is talking about the "wild blue yonder," you've already packed your bag!

When you are vibrating at a lower energy level, you may be non-committal, unreliable, and directionless. Forming meaningful relationships and becoming proficient in life skills are difficult, because you have an uncontrollable thirst for freedom and change. You are easily distracted and let life take you where it will, while doing unimportant things that lack purpose. To you it is more about the process than the finished product. In retrospect, this number realizes it should have spent more time planning. If your life path number is five, then you are an adventurer, craving and thriving on upbeat situations. If you don't learn to commit, you run the risk of having an unfulfilling life.

The number five card in tarot is The Hierophant, who advocates for learning. The zodiac that best resembles the energy of a number five is Leo energy, who is an energetic force that embraces enjoyment and expression. Virgo and Gemini energy are also associated with this sign because of their curiosity.

In shadow you may feel stuck, most likely due to your fear of commitment to relationships, jobs, or a way of life. Your excessive need for freedom manifests in every aspect of your life. Learn to find a balance between freedom and security.

Number Six

The number six is about being heart centered and of service to others. It represents unconditional love and the ability to support, nurture, and heal. When you embrace this energy, the people in your emotional partnerships will open up, let their guards down, and be more honest about their feelings. This allows you to understand and appreciate the needs of others. Work with this powerful energy when you need more compassion and hope.

The strengths of number six are being supportive and protective, loving, warm, nurturing, and charming. You likely have a close-knit circle of friends. When you need a shoulder to lean on, a six truly listens and seeks to understand. You value peace and truth and are always equipped with a kind, soft presence and heartfelt advice. The protective nature of a six uses unconditional love to speak for those who don't have a voice. Its romantic nature is only happy when its partner is also happy, so it puts in the effort to make that so. Your sense of togetherness is deeply important to you.

When you are vibrating at a lower energy level, you may be passive, self-sacrificing, and idealistic. You have the propensity to lose yourself and get taken advantage of, and even overpowered. You will sacrifice yourself at the expense of others and have the idea that if everyone were like you, the world would be perfect. If your life path number is six, you were blessed with a huge heart to nurture and protect others with. Your life lesson may be to realize the importance of self-love and acknowledge that your own needs are just as important as others'—it's a process that gains strength over time.

The tarot card that best reflects this energy is The Lovers, as it is a card that represents love and partnership and the efforts required to make them work. The zodiac signs associated with the energy of the number six are Virgo, Taurus, and Libra, because of their service-oriented nature that desires devotion.

In shadow, your nature of taking care of people may lean toward overly controlling a situation, and if you give too much (whether asked to do so or not), you will become resentful. Your generous nature and willingness to make a huge sacrifice for your family sometimes makes you lose sight of your own needs, wants, and desires. Please remember, it is okay to take care of yourself first.

Number Seven

Seven is deep and wise, having no time for frivolous things. When you need to dig deep into the heart of the matter and search for awareness, this energy helps you ask the right questions, research, and listen. This is all intellect, as seven is not emotional. This energy will help you find enjoyment in gathering and filtering through information and raw data to find answers you seek. As you search for answers, you are also strengthening your intuition. This combination of conscious and subconscious thinking will take you to the very deepest realms to access hidden truths.

The strengths of number seven are being spiritual, curious, and analytical. You are intelligent, intuitive, and love research. You need tangible evidence before you believe anything or take action and may come across as a "know it all." There's an air of mystery about a seven, something you can't quite figure out. Your quest is to set off on a path of self-development to help you find answers to deep and meaningful questions. These people are introverted and only have one or two deep friendships—most acquaintances tend to be shallow. While religion is too limiting for this boundless number, a very personal, intellectual, and deep connection to the spiritual world gives its experience in this life more mystery and meaning. It seeks to find and absorb as much knowledge and understanding as it can. The methodical nature of this number allows it to separate what is useful from what is meaningless to increase its wisdom.

When you are vibrating at a lower energy level, you may be reclusive, secretive, skeptical, and suspicious. All of your learning and seeking of truth and knowledge may limit your actual life experiences. You become mysterious and guarded, making it impossible to genuinely connect to others. Your inner circle might be few, and your friends tend to be more eccentric. If your life path number is seven, then you are inquisitive; however, you tend to be a solitary creature who fears relationships and vulnerability.

The tarot card associated with the number seven is The Chariot, which is about going on a quest. You use focus and intention to quickly drive toward your purpose. The zodiacs most associated with this number are Libra and Pisces, because of the energy of unwavering truth of Libra and the spiritual nature of Pisces.

In shadow, without a strong foundation rooted in spirituality, you could become jaded and cynical. Seek a higher power, no matter what form, and stay grounded. Strive to enjoy the beauty of nature and live near a body of water.

Number Eight

Number eight is about achievement, measuring life by the goals you reach, as this energy comes with a strong drive for success. It is also about balance, as you can see by its symmetrical shape. For every blessing you receive, the energy of this number will put a blessing back in the universe for someone else. Having a sense of balance brings feelings of stability, control, and support. This number works well with root chakra work. Eight is about infinity and attracting—manifestation is boundless. This energy represents the ultimate form of achievement that many will spend their entire lives striving for.

The strengths of number eight are being ambitious, karmic, and enduring. You are on a mission, and you like to achieve. With every accomplishment you gain more energy to push forward, but your assets may come at a significant personal cost. You are a visionary who can see their success and make it a reality. You are balanced in the fact that you know success is all about giving back, as well as recognizing and appreciating those who helped you.

When you are vibrating at a lower energy level, you may be materialistic, authoritative, and entitled. Your accomplishments may go to your head, and some may see you as shallow because you dismiss others and their efforts quickly. You may lose support as fast as you obtain it because you do not ask for permission or forgiveness. An eight life path struggles the most with taking advice. Because you are used to getting your way, you would be served well by working on teamwork. If your life path number is eight, you may often find great success in life. This has nothing to do with luck; it's because of your hard work and determination. You may excel professionally, but keep your ego in check.

In tarot, this number is associated with The Strength card, representative of karmic power and careful influence. The zodiac signs associated with this number are Scorpio and Capricorn because they hold the same strength and resolve as this number. Also, Capricorn energy is ruled by Saturn, the planet of karma and hard work.

In shadow you will not feel safe without financial success and material gain. However, your pursuit of attaining material wealth may lead to losing sight of the bigger picture. Due to the nature of a figure eight, you may experience many highs and many lows. If you are experiencing an exceptionally low point, remember that your good luck will return soon. Be patient.

Number Nine

Number nine is about completion but not finality because everything is energy and works in cycles. When you see nine in repeating patterns, the universe is helping you transition from one thing to another. The universe knows you have gone through your share of hardships and encourages you to become stronger and wiser in spite of your burdens. The energy of transformation guides and empowers with its wisdom. When you are ready to release and grow, you become more compassionate, kind, and able to provide support to others who are now where you were.

What makes a life path number of nine incredibly special is that it holds the qualities of all the other numbers, giving it a strong energetic vibration. The strengths of number nine are awakening, tolerance, and support, with a healing quality to it. The number nine represents the value and magnitude of inner wisdom and helps others to awaken to their higher selves. You see the injustices in the world, and you want to fix them all because your main goal is to make the world a better place. This energy handles leadership with grace and tolerance because of its ability to extend space and respect to everyone. You may always find yourself in leadership roles, even if you don't ask for it.

When you are vibrating at a lower energy level, you may be resentful, sacrificing, and suffer greatly. Some of your life experiences have left a heavy imprint on your heart, and you may not have taken the time to heal your own wounds. As you work to help others at the cost or your own energy work, you create a sacrificial mindset that can fall into a life of lack and suffering. If your life path number is nine, you are a humanitarian at heart, supporting all for the greatest good. Make sure you do Moon work to release past pains and learn your own value and worth.

The ninth tarot card, associated to the number nine, is The Hermit—reflective of your same qualities. In astrology, Sagittarius and Aries energy are associated with the number nine because they capture your expansive, philosophical, and open-minded nature with a willingness to endure any challenge.

In shadow you become so busy with your leadership roles that you don't always nurture your deeply spiritual side that needs to be introspective to heal old wounds. If you are carrying around old wounds, please learn to let go of the past and let artistic and creative outlets stir your soul. You may be somewhat gullible because of your idealistic nature— remember that not everyone's true nature is as noble as yours.

Number Eleven

Master number eleven (life path number) provides you with a stronger energetic vibration than most numbers. You are the empath and deeply intuitive, and you are on a unique spiritual journey in this lifetime. The energy of this number is charismatic, inventive, and idealistic. You rely more on faith than logic and reasoning, and you have a well-developed sense of morality.

When you are vibrating at a lower energy level, you may experience anxiety or depression. Because you are sensitive to the emotions of others, it's important to take care of yourself while helping others. Spend time staring at the sky, learning astrology, tarot, and more about numerology. Growing into the power and strength of the number eleven can be difficult, and you may have started off life under difficult circumstances.

The trials of your life have made you wiser, so you can solve problems effectively through solid judgement. Material things don't interest you much. Rather, you're attracted to philosophy, a quest for enlightenment, and healing. The energy of any master number can be overpowering, and your well-developed sensitivity can throw you off balance. Make sure you put a lot of energy and focus into your physical body and by extension your environment. A peaceful life is meaningful and important to you.

Number Twenty-Two

Master number twenty-two (life path number) is considered the master builder. You are magnetic in attracting all that you need to manifest your deepest desires and leave a positive and remarkable impact on this world in some way. You are a true visionary that can turn your ideas into reality. Most likely your vision is about the greater good, due to this number's humanitarian side. Someone with this life path number is responsible, intuitive, and knowledgeable. You are powerful and also possess the same practical aptitude as a number four.

Some people with this number waste their ability due to their practical nature. You struggle with the fear of failure, burdened by the knowledge of your own potential. Learn to trust yourself enough to take risks because you truly know if an idea has potential from the beginning. You will be scrutinized by others, possibly out of envy. Don't let that get to you.

Number Thirty-Three

Master number thirty-three (life path number) is the master teacher and most spiritually evolved of all numbers. It exemplifies the nurturing and loving qualities of soul-urge number six. You have a loyal and understanding nature with active listening skills. You strive to see the good in others and tend to forgive easily. You may struggle as you grow into your skills. Your abilities may not fully manifest until you are in your mid-thirties, and even with that, you must be open to them.

Numbers can show up in your birth date or can be representative of the letters in your name. Anywhere you see these numbers means you have the energy of those numbers within you, or the universe is lending you a helping hand by loaning those attributes to you or bringing people into your life to help you expand into those characteristics. Where it appears in your chart reading will provide you with more clues as to how its meaning plays out in your life. No matter what, a one is powerful and will stop at nothing to achieve its dreams, a two brings in the energy of harmony, a three blesses you with positive energy and creative expression, a four expresses the energy of determination, dependability, and wisdom within you, a five brings adventurous influence, a six is filled with warmth and kindness, a seven brings wise and spiritual energy, an eight brings about opportunity and abundance, and finally, the number nine is a force of kindness, compassion, and wisdom within you.

Numerology Journey

Numerology is more in-depth than what I have just described, because numbers have a spiritual meaning, which can be interpreted as advice, predictions, and insight. If you keep seeing repeating numbers, look them up. Repeating numbers, such as 111 and 444, are an amplification of energy. The more a particular number shows up around you, the more the meaning or vibration behind the number is influencing you (or trying to influence you). If the repeating numbers are something such as the birthday of a loved one you've lost, the synchronicity could mean that they just want you to know they are near. My sister, Lara, and I often see the numeric pattern 1121 in the strangest of places. This number is my brother, David's, birthday—November 21. I always get a warm feeling, like he's giving me a big energetic bear hug, when I see those numbers. The more you grow on your spiritual journey and learn to trust your intuition, the more you will notice patterns of repeating numbers and letters.

My sister was in tune with her spiritual side long before me. I used to harass her, as is my nature of being the baby in the family, and this was before I completely connected to my inner goddess power. One time we were on a road trip, and along the way we passed a Taco Bell, I shouted out, "Lara, look, I see two L's!" Of course, we were all laughing, and it was in good fun. I share this little story with you to mention an important point... If those around you are not in-tune with their spiritual side, then they just won't understand... and that's okay. As you experience more synchronicities and unlock your spiritual gifts, you may want to keep it to yourself until you attract a tribe that understands you. Not everyone will be able to go on this journey with you.

Much like astrology, you can use numerology to unlock the intricate details about who you are and provide a framework on which you can build your life. You can start to understand why you struggle with some things in your life, while other things come so naturally. It can reveal your life's purpose and help you feel safe in the knowledge that your shortcomings are just learning opportunities to direct you on the right path. At its very core, numerology helps you understand who you are so you can work with your energy and overcome any barriers that you may face.

Whether you are new to studying numbers or just beginning your spiritual quest, be ready for change. Numerology can help you learn how to emphasize your strengths and overcome your weaknesses. Actually, it can pretty much tell you everything about you. Almost anything you need to know can be found within the vibrational patterns of numbers. As your energy begins to shift, the energy of the universe will bring you new opportunities, unravel a new career path, and bring new people into your life. The messages can show up numerically or in any other form. As you begin to see and experience more synchronicities, you may wonder, "Were these signs here all along and I was just blind to them?" You have to be open to it to experience it. The thing that differentiates synchronicity from coincidence is meaning, like with seeing my brother's birthday. Remember that you will have to learn new things on this journey but also unlearn old patterns. The numbers you see may remind you of this as well. The study of numerology ultimately leads to self-realization, conscious manifestation, and healing. See the exercises in Chapter Nine to start your quest!

6

OTHER ENERGETIC INFLUENCES

Divine Influences

Outside of following lunar cycles and knowing about the Sun, astrology, planets, houses, and numbers, there are still so many fascinating ways to incorporate energy work. In this chapter you will learn about animal energy, God/Goddess energy, and angelic energy that can influence your spiritual work. Influence is about unseen forces that help to create visible results with lasting effects on your character and behavior. All energy work is about collaborating energetically with spiritual entities, or some conduit for Source energy, which some people refer to as divine. You can harness any energy from above to help you use their qualities in your life and aid in your energetic healing process.

Animal Energy

Animals cannot speak as humans do, but if you are a pet lover, you know that communication is possible with a different kind of language, one of spirit and energy, which can be uniquely pure and profound. Animals can notice your vibe quickly. Collaborating with spirit animal energy deepens not only your energy work but also your connection with the natural world. By connecting with a particular archetypal spiritual essence of a particular animal, this energy can help awaken amazing and powerful qualities that may have been lying dormant within you. What you want to do is connect with the spiritual and energetic frequency of that species of animal.

Pay attention to animals that show up for you. Notice their qualities to see what value they present. Native Americans have animal symbols associated with the zodiac. For those that believe, we all have a power animal that stays with us for life, but there can be others that correspond with different levels of our own consciousness. You can choose an animal energy to work with, or it may very well choose you. Pay attention to animals that present themselves to you. Owning a pet isn't the same thing as a spiritual animal encounter. Although, the animals you choose to have in your life have meaning too. The significance of having pets and how you treat them speaks loudly about your personal character and what you value and prioritize in your life.

The way animals present themselves to you doesn't have to be in their natural habitat. They can present in photos, ads... Don't discount anything you see. Work with your third eye to see hidden meanings in your experiences. Working with animal energy is the same as any other. You use intention, sit with the energy by looking at a photo of a particular animal, holding your gaze, meditate on it, and ask that its true nature be revealed to you. You can work with animal tarot or oracle decks to discover their powerful medicine. There is no right or wrong way to work with spiritual energy; it is a personal experience, unique to everyone.

Some animal encounters may not be about their energy but bringing your attention to something else entirely—a personalized message, if you will. A particular experience of mine happened at a cemetery on Memorial Day weekend in the United States. I always decorate my brother's grave, and also Greg's, a man I never knew, but who is buried next to him. I had a box of little flags, and I walked through the cemetery, placing a flag near any headstone that indicated military. I was about thirty minutes in, when out of nowhere I was covered in ladybugs. I looked around and noticed they were all over the headstones and grave markers. I was afraid to move. I, all of a sudden, felt happy and just started laughing. Lady bugs bring positive messages and good fortune with them. My interpretation of this encounter was that all the spirits in the cemetery were thanking me for what I was doing.

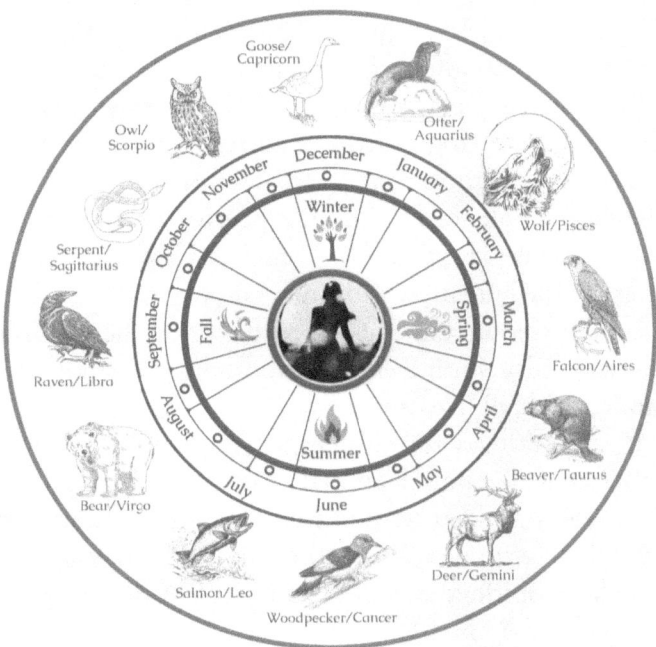

Native Americans have animal symbols associated with the zodiac. The beaver is in the east and associated with spring, as it is a master builder and creator. This is the time of the new moon energy, when you begin to establish what you want in your life. The raven, a trickster, is in the west and associated with fall. This is the time of the full moon and shadow work, when your ego can express characteristics of the raven and deceive even you. You can research the symbolism with these animals to see how their meanings tie in with other energies discussed in this book.

Lunar animals mimic the moon's qualities, such as cycles of time, psyche, balance, and mystery. When you research animal spirits or animal totems, you can decide for yourself which ones emulate moon-like qualities. The moon with its mothering qualities acts as a guiding light in darkness, providing nocturnal creatures with all of the skills and gifts that they require to survive and thrive. The wolf has extreme heightening of all of its senses due to its nocturnal nature. I love to mimic its loyalty to La Luna as I howl at a full moon! The moon bestowed the bat with intellectual gifts, while a wise old owl enjoys intuitive gifts. The dolphin is playful and generous, displaying qualities of grace, while the frog portrays transformation, symbolizing attainment of enlightenment and contentment. The moon is also the ruler of all aquatic animals because of its association with water. Every lunar animal possesses its own spiritual meaning, divine guidance, and timely messages that reflect the qualities of the moon. Lunar creatures teach you the importance of maternal and feminine energies and how important it is to be in touch with all five of your senses.

As it is working with all energy, you should thank your spirit messenger or power animal when it shows up. Always take a moment and express gratitude from your heart center. As a Reiki practitioner, I send healing Reiki to the animal messenger, the spirit energy of the animal I worked with, or to Gaia herself.

Goddess Energy

The cover of my book fittingly pictures a depiction of Artemis, Greek goddess of the moon. Her connection with her brother, Apollo, god of the Sun, is unique because their energy creates balance in their relationship. They are fraternal twins of Leto and Zeus and share many similarities, such as prowess in hunting.[13] But, their differences are literally night and day. This book does not delve into forming a connection or relationship with any specific deity; rather, I write about being introspective and finding this energy within. If you are looking to form a connection with a deity, simply sit in stillness as you visualize a specific deity showing up for you, and patiently wait and listen for a message. Connecting with nature to be at one with Gaia, Mother Earth, helps to access divine energy within.

Goddess energy is simply another term for feminine energy and is not gender based. The parts of us that embody feminine principles such as intuition, compassion, reception, reflection, sensuality, and wisdom come from Goddess energy. When you are gentle but fierce, easygoing but powerful, capable, embody strength, a student and the teacher, and spontaneous yet wise, you are expressing attributes of the divine feminine archetype. It is an energetic flow that embraces being and receiving. Earlier in this book I described divine feminine energy as negative, receptive, passive energy. Goddess energy is more about love, compassion, and intuition, rather than the innovation, creativity, and willpower of the divine masculine energy.

The source of life itself comes from feminine energy, because of its cyclical and fertile nature. It is complex and spiritual, allowing you to connect to your inner world. Think of Gaia, Mother Earth, and all the life that springs forth from her. You too have that power inside of you; you only need to harness

---

[13] Dani Rhys, "Apollo and Artemis – Greek Mythology," https://symbolsage.com/apollo-and-artemis-mythology/.

it. Accessing this energy in today's busy world can be difficult, as it requires rest and stillness, which is necessary so you can receive (feminine) rather than produce or create (masculine). There's immense power in stillness, as it allows you to access your inner spark so you can freely express yourself. Of course, you need to find your yin-yang balance between activity and stillness, giving and receiving, and creating and resting. It is in balance where you find yourself in great health mentally, physically, and spiritually.

Feminine energy is also about connecting to your intuition, your inner knowledge, without intellect, reason, or proof, and comes from your heart center. This also implies the need for stillness, because if your mind is too busy, your heart cannot express itself. When you allow your heart to direct your energy, you will slowly start to hear the influence of your intuition. There are components of faith and trust in developing your intuition. You must learn to trust yourself through your thoughts, words, and actions. Is your inner voice protecting you—thereby holding you back—or is it speaking authentically to inspire you? By connecting to divine feminine energy, you create balance with masculine energy. You need masculine energy to manifest your dreams, but without balance you can fall into depression or addiction. Society has conditioned you to hold back your feelings, deny them, and carry on—which is predominately living a life through masculine energy. Living like this only creates negative emotional energy stores in your body, which creates mental and physical pain. When you feel your feelings, you are honoring Goddess energy in its raw form—this is healthy.

Connecting with Goddess energy is also about honoring your spiritual nature, which needs to grow, evolve, and ascend. By creating a daily practice that compliments you and what you are creating in this life and finding time to surround yourself with nature, you will create an energetic harmony that's pure magic. You express goddess characteristics when you do such acts as selflessly taking care of others, but this energy is also about the love, care, gentleness, and compassion you devote to yourself. Bond with your body. Taking care of your physical body and inner sanctum is a way to respect your inner goddess. Your body is full of wisdom, so connecting to that inner flame of divinity allows you to release unexpressed emotions and trauma, which is vital to living your best life.

So, smile at a stranger, feed the birds, eat healthy, and release negative thoughts. Treat people how you wish to be treated, but make sure you practice self-care so you know how it feels to be loved. Devote sacred time to a daily ritual that helps grow your inner essence. It's not about the amount of time and the activity of your ritual, but just make sure you make time for some "me time," where you create a safe space so your inner self can feel and express. Tuning into your Goddess energy is a process that takes time, so don't rush. Take one day at a time. Eventually, you will be able to honor your inner goddess in every moment through your thoughts and actions.

Lunar Deities

A lunar deity or moon goddess is a deity who represents the moon, or a specific aspect of the moon. Their functions are depicted through different traditions and cultures, of which there are similarities. When working with the moon, you may wish to incorporate specific Goddess energy for each astrological sign. There are many, and some go by different names, but to get you started on the path of incorporating goddess energy into your Moon work, I've chosen the following.

Aries: Athena

Aries is the first zodiac sign that marks the beginning of the astrological year, reflects the collective energy of the new moon, reveals the start of springtime, and commences a new cycle of life. In Greek mythology, Aries is fittingly called "the head," and the goddess Athena sprung fully formed from Zeus' head; therefore, she is associated with intellect.[14] The element of fire sparks raw creative thought in the mind, and the owl reflects her wisdom.

Taurus: Hathor

Hathor was one of the oldest goddesses in the Egyptian pantheon. Her name literally means "House of Horus," which can be interpreted by taking *house* and translating it to *womb*. In ancient Egyptian religion, Hathor is the goddess of the sky, women, motherhood, fertility, and love. She's a complex goddess with a vital role as mother. She was not only known for her mothering qualities, such as childbirth, protection, love, fertility, beauty, and pleasure, but also in consort she is the goddess of music and dancing.[15] She is mainly depicted with a cow head. The cow is a symbol of fertility, strength, and abundance. The spirit of the cow is profoundly mothering and a sign that all will be okay.

Gemini: Saraswati

Saraswati is the Hindu goddess of knowledge, music, art, speech, wisdom, and learning. She is depicted in images as a beautiful and graceful goddess, wearing spotless white apparel, seated on a lotus seat symbolizing light, knowledge,

---

[14] Carlos Albuquerque, "The Twelve Olympians in the Zodiac," https://mullerornis. medium.com/the-twelve-olympians-in-the-zodiac-303790337412#:~:text= Aries%20is%20associated%20with%20the%20head%2C%20and%20anyone,all %20traits%20intrinsic%20to%20Athena%20in%20her%20myths.

[15] Kelly Macquire, "Hathor the Egyptian Goddess of Love, Beauty and Pleasure," https://www.worldhistory.org/video/2781/hathor-the-egyptian-goddess-of-love-beauty-and-ple/.

and truth, with her many hands in mudra.[16] She is part of a trinity necessary to create, maintain, and regenerate/recycle the universe. When you work with her energy, incorporate the energy of the number three. This goddess represents the free flow of wisdom, the personification of knowledge relating to arts, sciences, crafts, and skills. So, if you need a boost to your creative center, working with her energy will help.

Cancer: Diana

Diana—the Huntress—is a Roman goddess equivalent to Greek Artemis. Diana goes by many names, including Queen of Heaven, Lunar Virgin, and Mother of Animals—in Italy she was Queen of the Witches, meaning wise women healers. When she ascended to Earth, she taught magick, and witches were born. Diana's proud and fierce power is best understood by looking at the violence surrounding her birth story. Despite her brutal beginning, this goddess reminds us to never forget the wonders of creation, the responsibility of being alive, and the importance of being a woman! Pray to her for courage, asking the universe to fill you with her strength to survive any challenge and change from within.[17]

Leo: Medusa

Medusa was the daughter of sea gods, making her Goddess of the Sea. She was portrayed as a scary creature with snakes for hair, but her energy is positive, invoking energy of protection. Specifically, she is a protector of women, as

---

[16] Temple Purohit, "Goddess Saraswati – Hindu Goddesses and Deities," https://www.templepurohit.com/hindu-goddesses-and-deities/goddess-saraswati-hindu-goddesses-and-deities/.

[17] Diana Esbats, "Goddess Diana," https://www.covenofthegoddess.com/goddess-diana/.

she would turn any man who dared stare at her into stone. Petrification, or turning into stone, is related to things that are motionless, but for Wild Moon Healing, I will define it as being emotionally numb, unfeeling, or closed off. It could also be interpreted as unresponsive in terms of taking action or adapting to change. Why work with her energy, which seems so cold? It is said that Medusa survived an assault by Poseidon, and her snakes were a gift from Athena for protection. Fittingly, she's become a symbol of female empowerment, releasing the downtrodden and oppressed. If you are feeling indifferent, get yourself some sea water or sea glass and ask her to empower you.

Virgo: Ceres

Ceres is the goddess of the harvest in Roman mythology, and was represented as a noble woman appearing majestic, tall, matronly, and dignified. She is associated with wheat and grain... Ever wonder why processed grain is called cereal? She is sometimes depicted with a cornucopia, symbolizing abundance. She was not only known for harvest and grain, but she taught the meek, mortal humans how to preserve and prepare corn grain. She is strongly rooted in earth energy, through agriculture fertility. If you have a negative relationship with food, Ceres' energy may help you to change how you associate food with feelings.

Libra: Lakshmi

Lakshmi is the Hindu goddess of good luck and fortune. She is always wearing pink, a color associated with tranquility, love, unity, harmony, beauty, and emotional healing. She usually holds a water pot (remember that water is a divine gift) and a pink or blue lotus. Blue can mean healing emotional wounds. She is the goddess of wealth and prosperity in material and spiritual form, but you need to have a goal and work toward it before she will energetically help you. It's said that she does not visit the lazy or unclean, as her energy is highly active.[18] If you are doing some "spring cleaning" in the fall, Lakshmi energy can help with decluttering your physical, mental, and emotional space.

Scorpio: Kali

Kali is a complex Hindu goddess of death and sexuality. She's considered to be the goddess of ultimate power, time, destruction, and change. She is referred to as the goddess of death or doomsday, or the black goddess. She symbolizes female empowerment and sexual liberation.[19] Scorpio and Kali both are about transformation, death, and sex. Kali is feminine energy, but not motherly. Transformation is hard, but, in the midst of change, Kali's energy can help you create the condition of strength, vitality, and energy from which new life can be generated.

Sagittarius: Fortuna

Fortuna is a Roman goddess of fortune and luck and regarded as the bearer of prosperity. It is said that she will impart you with divine wisdom and energy to aid you in your desire to create more wealth, health, and joy. The word "chance" is used a lot when describing her because she would randomly bless people and is sometimes depicted wearing a blindfold or spinning a wheel.[20] This indicates no prejudice

---

[18] Temple Purohit, "Goddess Lakshmi – Hindu Goddesses and Deities," https://www.templepurohit.com/hindu-goddesses-and-deities/goddess-lakshmi-hindu-goddesses-and-deities/.

[19] Wendy Doniger, "Kali," https://www.britannica.com/topic/Kali.

[20] Mike Greenberg, "Fortuna: Goddess of Luck in Rome," https://mythologysource.com/fortuna-goddess-of-luck/.

in giving fortune, and the fact that you can have good or bad luck, which is the way life goes. There isn't much data about her online, but she does bless the land in the United States around the time Thanksgiving is celebrated. The lack of information about her makes me feel that she is just as mysterious as the moon.

Capricorn: Juno

Another Roman goddess, Juno, equivalent of Greek Hera, was chief goddess and female counterpart of Jupiter, equivalent of Greek Zeus, known for spirituality and expansion. Juno was queen of the Roman gods, and her spouse, Jupiter, was king of the gods. She sounds like queen mother, as she protects and champions for women, especially in domestic roles of marriage and motherhood. She was respected, depicted wearing a tunic, a veil, or crown, and holding a libation bowl.[21] She was often depicted with a peacock, an animal with deep spiritual meaning of renewing the soul, freedom from worry, balance, harmony, spiritual enlightenment, and connection to the divine.

Aquarius: Isis

Isis is one of the most important goddesses in ancient Egypt. She was a universal goddess that could influence the cosmos with her magical powers, which is why some called her the great magician. She is the female archetype for creation and came to fulfill feminine roles such as wife, mother, mourner, and magical healer.[22] She's the role model for women in a traditional sense. Invoke her energy for healing and nurturing.

---

[21] Thomas Aple, "Roman Goddess Juno," https://mythopedia.com/topics/juno.
[22] Alphabet.net, "Goddess ISIS: Symbol, Meaning, Facts and Images," https://www.alphapedia.net/goddess-isis/.

Pisces: Kuan Yin

Kuan Yin is a goddess of compassion. The Buddhas say she is related to "woman's work" because she brings boundless love and comfort to all people and could ease the inevitable pains of human life.[23] This archetype has no equal. Just like Pisces, she is symbolized with fish, because of the great depths of her motherly, healing energy that evoke the ocean.

Divine Spiritual Guides

Have you ever experienced a coincidence too eerie to explain, been struck by an intense sense of intuition, or had a dream that helped you with your current experience? When this happens, it could be your spirit guide(s) trying to influence you or draw your attention to something specific. A spirit guide is an incarnate spirit that guides and protects a living embodied individual—they are entities that provide us with spiritual guidance. On the earthly plain, we often speak of the importance of having a strong community to support us and add meaning to our lives. But the connections that empower us aren't limited to the mortal realm. The energetic network discussed in this book is incredibly powerful, and you have your personal team that you can harness for support at any time. Some guides are with you from birth to death, while others come and go at certain times of your life, based on the experience you have at that time. You can freely request or invoke other spirit guides as you wish (see the Using Energy section in Chapter Seven for more about invocation). While there are varying interpretations of spirit guides out there, most of them fit into several overarching categories, such as

---

[23] Liz Turnbull, "Kuan Yin: Goddess of Compassion," https://goddessgift.com/goddesses/kuan-yin/.

archangels, guardian angels, spirit animals, ascended masters, departed loved ones (anyone from your ancestral line), or higher angels.

Angels are messengers of God. While angel energy is of God (or Source), there are many types of energy discussed in this book that do not require faith in a creator. As Friedrich Nietzsche said, "There are no facts, only interpretations." Your source is personal to you; it can mean many things and present in various ways.

All angels, guardian angels, and archangels correspond with people on various frequencies. The difference between an angel and an archangel is that God created archangels for specific reasons, such as Saint Gabriel, who was conceived to deliver news to Mary that she was to bear the messiah. Archangels are leaders in the angel world, holding a powerful, exceptionally large energetic signature. The prefix *arch* is used to denote *chief,* so they are chief messengers of God. These powerful guides have specific gifts and can work with many different humans at one time.

- Archangel Michael is the protector and defender,
- Gabriel is the messenger,
- Raphael is the healer of physical illness,
- Uriel (or Ariel) is the pillar of divine strength,
- Jophiel is the giver of joy,
- Chamuel is the peacekeeper, and
- Zadkiel is the guide of life paths.

There are other types of angels, such as the Angel of Death (Azrael), and other rank-and-file angels, such as Cherubim, who guards against sin. There are seraphim, six-winged angels that sing without ceasing and are associated with light and purity. Principalities and powers are demons and include fallen angels such as Lucifer. A caution that working with demonic entities to confuse, frustrate, or worse, to harm any other person may karmatically come back to you three-fold. There is no positive angle to working with these spirits. Any type of angel can be invoked at any time, as they all are fighting a spiritual war that surrounds us all. You can call on them when you need them; they are always here. They assist with bringing the light within the mind of God and love from within the heart of God into the hearts and minds of us all in order to positively affect our will. As they do their jobs, we, one by one, are filled with love and become light workers and energy healers.

While there are many good spirits to connect to and work with, you need to protect yourself against bad spirits at the same time. No spirit can cause you physical harm, but the voice of an evil spirit can sound like your subconscious and put things in your mind that are not true and influence you to act against your true nature. They also create a dense, low-vibrational energy in your environment that makes it harder for you to release what you need to and hear the guidance of good spirits. If you feel lost and miserable, you may want to consider trying to remove negative spirits. You can simply tell them, "Be gone. You are not needed here." What I frequently do to protect my energy is smudge sage over myself and my home and crack a window so the bad energy leaves with the smoke as it flows out through the window.

I read about an interesting visualization to rid yourself of negative influences by tricking them into thinking you are gone. Therefore, they leave. If you work with entities and feel that a negative spirit is trying to connect with you or interfere with your life in some way, try this rendition of what I read about:

Invisibility Cloak Visualization

Sit somewhere you are comfortable, with your feet on the floor or lying down. Focus on your breath, breathing in and out of your nose (or mouth if that's more comfortable for you). In your mind's eye, begin to imagine yourself where you are in this exact moment; see your room, your home, your neighborhood, or your town... Make the scope as big as you want. See the negative entities that are around you. You might see dark figures, smog... Whatever you see is your intuition at work. Then, see yourself in your mind's eye. Snap your fingers, and poof—all of a sudden, everything disappears, except for the bad spirits.

Imagine them looking dumbfounded and confused because you disappeared. Watch them leave because they can no longer see you or bother you, or anyone else for that matter. When you are certain they are gone, snap your fingers to unveil your invisibility cloak. You and everything around you return to normal and you feel how the energy around you has changed. This energetic shift should help you to experience a state of happiness and joy that the negative entities were previously attacking. Bring these positive feelings back into the present moment.

Sometimes your ancestors divinely come to visit in challenging times or present themselves when you are in the deepest depth of your healing work. During breathwork, I've seen my ancestors and other spirits many times. One time my Nan Nan sat with me during a breathwork class, and before she left, she stood outside of the barn where the class was held and took the time to smoke a Pall Mall. She told me, "I don't know what you youngins are doing, but I like it!" It was the encouragement I needed at that time to keep me on my healing journey.

Another time, during breathwork, a man sat cross legged next to me. He said, "You don't know me, but I'm your Uncle Herman. Keep it up. You are healing all of us." Afterward, I found pictures of him. He presented to me as a young man and exactly as he looked in the black and white photographs. His reassurance was comforting.

One time, before I began my spiritual journey, I was sitting on my stairs crying, as I was in the middle of a horrible situation. For the first time, I really felt my late brother's presence since he had passed. A coldness overtook the room, I could see my breath, and I smelled his cologne—Obsession. I heard his voice in my head say, "Nothing you can do now, so get out of your head." I felt a huge angelic hug, and just like that, I stopped crying. I was young when he passed away. He was my protector, always making me feel safe, and through this encounter, it was like he took my pain away.

I'll share one more story, a true testimony of influences from above. I was thirteen when I lost my brother. I was the baby of the family, and everyone treated me like one—as if I didn't understand what had happened. I grew up in an atmosphere of "get over it" and "life goes on," and when I tried to speak, I was pushed off. "Not now, Donna. Just go to your room." It was just another part of my childhood that reinforced the false belief that I wasn't important. My room became my prison. For six months, I cursed God aloud, screaming obscenities in His name. How could He need my brother more than me? The nerve of Him! I became so lost in my pain that I sobbed every night. I would change my night shirt one or two times each night because they were so drenched with my tears. I barely slept. One night I just couldn't take it anymore. I didn't want to die, but I didn't know how to live. I went to my brother's room that was untouched, as if he was still going to come home. I opened the chest at the end of his bed where he kept his guns. But, the guns were gone. Divine wisdom had my father pick them up about two days prior, and I didn't know. So, I did the only thing I could think of. I apologized. I sat at my window looking up at the moon and I said, just as loudly as I cursed him, "I'm sorry. Please help save me from me." Not knowing if I was heard, I just crawled into bed. The next morning was a beautiful spring-like day in February, and I actually heard birds chirping outside my window. As I stretched, I realized... I fell asleep as soon as my head hit the pillow and hadn't shed one tear. What a wonderful celestial gift! I only slept a couple of hours a night, if at all, for months. I was so tired, and God saw that I needed rest. I've never thought of harming myself again since that day, but I still lived in a grieved status for many years.

God, the universe, higher self, whatever you call your Source, has love that is personal. They know you as an individual and love you personally and unconditionally. There is no beginning or end to divine love. In personally experiencing divine love, it didn't matter what I had said or what I had done prior to dropping to my knees, staring out my window, and apologizing to anyone who was listening. All was forgiven; no shame or guilt for my actions remained. Working with divine spiritual guides comes with absolutely no judgement. There is no human feeling or experience like having divine spiritual guidance because human beings all have preconceived notions, opinions, inherited beliefs, and judgement.

To collaborate with spirit guides, you must be present in your everyday life to receive their messages. Often times guides reach out at the most opportune time, but we are too busy, so their message is lost. Starting a gratitude journal will help you to become more appreciative for all things, which will welcome divine spirits and more gifts for you to treasure into your life. Just as guides know you individually, you should get to know them. See if a name comes to you from one of your guides via your intuition, through meditation, or synchronicity. If not, get creative and give them a name to encourage them to connect with you more regularly. Further your knowledge of them through online searches, books, classes, or workshops. Sometimes simply learning more about them magically opens you up to more communication. To get to know your guides I encourage you to practice meditation to improve your intuition and to develop a daily, weekly, or monthly spiritual practice. I may not journal every night, but I have rituals I perform with the energy from a new and full moon. You can add a divination tool, such as tarot or oracle cards, and use a pendulum or dowsing rods. The easiest way to communicate with them is through your thoughts—your thoughts create your reality. You can, in your mind, ask for guidance, help, or support. You can even use prayers or blessings. Just articulate your need. They are listening.

Spiritual Nature of Numbers

Rather than simply giving you numbers to learn more about yourself, as with numerology, or the definition of an angel number to guide, support, or encourage you, I also want to share with you the spiritual nature of numbers. Each digit holds a unique vibrational pattern (or archetype) that is a container for the currents of divine, universal life (prana) in which we all flow and that flows within us. Divinity of numbers is about creation of the world, and each and every life. The following sequence of numbers describe the path to enlightenment. The divine essence of numbers not only created the cosmos but provides the path of life, spirituality, and your existential existence. Numbers also describe the energetic network and how correspondences flow. Each number is an energetic building block to allow you to live your soul's purpose.

Zero

The number zero is a circle, where creative potential exists. It measures nothingness with immense power. This vortex of power has ideas circulating, yet nothing has tangible form. It's the beginning, and in the beginning there was nothing—complete darkness. Its power resembles the female womb energy of creation which designed the cosmos, and it created you. Gaia was created from darkness in chaos. God was created in nothing from his own greatness. The "god particle" exploded and created the universe. Whatever you believe, most can agree that some intelligence is behind all outer *seeming*. Notice I didn't write *seeing,* as in with your eyes or third eye. Its intelligence is professed, and it is pure potentiality.

One

One is the essence of singularity and identity because the ultimate objective is to be one with your higher self, God, or the universe. The number one is perfectly straight, like an arrow providing direction to the path of seeking, reaching, and exploring necessary to define your authenticity. Because of its singular essence, some ancient cultures did not view it as a number, as the word "number" indicates plurality; however, they believed it to be a source to all other numbers, because adding ones together creates whole numbers— in essence, it's the source that makes things whole. The Fibonacci sequence creates a spiral, starting mathematically with one plus one, and is seen in nature, human anatomy, art, and music. As John Brahier, a teacher of theology, stated in the *Journal of Catholic Education,* "Mathematics can reveal this beauty, which in turn reveals God."[24]

Two

Two provides union, balance, duality, and polarity. Two is the energetic vibration of yin and yang, and more specifically male and female, because the ultimate concept of manifestation is co-creation, as nothing is created by self alone. The exotic expression of union forms new life. In the Bible, the story of Noah includes two of every animal, male and female, so they could create more life once the

---

[24] John Brahier, "Beauty, Bees, and God: The Fibonacci Sequence as a Theological Springboard in Secondary Mathematics," extension://efaidnbmnnnibpcajpcglclefind mkaj/https://files.eric.ed.gov/fulltext/EJ1231335.pdf.

floods receded. There is more to creating than just new life. Creativity births new ideas, and ingenuity gives those ideas form. You are here to create in a way that only you can because there is only one of you, and there will never be another. Perhaps the greatest power in the number two is that it reminds you that you are not alone, and Source is sending all the vibrational energy you need to thrive and create a beautiful life.

Three

Three is the first real number where energy, flow, and motion begin to reveal unity. It's the second calculation in the Fibonacci sequence (1 + 2 = 3) which starts the curve (i.e., energetic flow). This realm of motion creates a harmonic rhythm, which is characterized by progression and position. In addition to divine energy in motion, there is also power in the divine energy of trinity. It is seen in so many concepts, such as maiden/mother/crone, mind/body/spirit, God the father/son/Holy Ghost, or even brain/heart/gut. Communication through the vast energetic network flows within your body, your being, and your seeming. It is the structure of energy flowing *as above, so below, flows within*. Tapping into this magical energy can activate positive thoughts, and it draws you back to self.

Four

Four creates sacred space or sanctuary within; therefore, it is the number of *being*. The essences of your values and beliefs connect the body/mind/soul to your physical world, which starts to create structure and organization. The more stable your foundation, the more your aura is nurtured and protected. This sanctuary within is where authenticity breeds, and where the communication between your mind, heart, and gut occurs. There is a divine reason your heart has four chambers, and I believe it is the temple for the soul, which is why you want to transmit energy from your heart center. The spiritual heart holds the notion of reverence to a higher power, or as an extension of one's higher self, and helps calm the mind and body, reflected through healthy heart regulation.[25]

Five

Five is an outward expression of manifestation, and its energy is free, curious, and creative. It represents the five elements of earth, air, water, fire, and spirit, which are the components necessary to imaginatively create. Human beings have five senses (sight, smell, touch, hearing, and taste) that allow us to experience the world. We also have five fingers on each hand and five toes on each foot to serve the same purpose. There are five pillars of Islam—declaration of faith, prayer, giving, fasting, and pilgrimage—and Muslims pray five times a day. This energy of five is alive and active, so five represents *doing,* as seen in concepts such as faith in action and a mindful connection to nature. You cannot experience the world authentically if you first do not master the ability to just be (the energy of number four).

Six

Six is about seeing in the form of your sixth sense, power of perception, and keen intuitive power. This number connects intuitive guides to your inner knowing. It represents the third eye and clairvoyance. Inner wisdom is a subconscious quality that can't distinguish vison from reality, but with

---

[25] Micheline Anderson, "The Spiritual Heart, A Scientific Inquiry," https://www. heartmath.org/articles-of-the-heart/spiritual-heart/.

inner vision you can form things in the mind that potentially can take hold in reality. In Christianity, man was created on the sixth day. The number six might refer to multitudes, meaning the people of Israel, and really all of humanity.[26] Your intuition is what brings you in contact with the collective unconsciousness within humanity's energetic field. The ultimate energy of six is love. And it is love that heals the collective.

Seven

Here is the realm of divine vibration, serendipity, and synchronicity that always guides you to the divine vibration of your higher self. It is perfection, a state that humans cannot sustain. In Christianity, the number seven looms large in the book of Revelation and all throughout the Old Testament. God created the heavens and the earth in seven days—it represents a full, complete, and perfect world. In the New Testament, seven symbolizes the unity of the four corners of the earth (cardinal directions) with the holy trinity. The Book of Proverbs lists actions that God disapproves of, which parallels the seven deadly sins (pride, envy, wrath, gluttony, lust, sloth, and greed). In Judaism, there are seven branches of the Menorah. But the significance of seven extends beyond divine belief. There are seven colors in a rainbow, seven musical notes, and Seven Wonders of the World. This number also represents the main chakras helping energy flow within you, and it signifies intuitive knowing, because when you are balanced, your energy can connect self to the divine. This vibration is what sends the red cardinal to you with

---

[26] Ned Walker, "The Spiritual Significance of the Number 6," https://bahaiteachings. org/spiritual-significance-number-6/.

a message, because the portal from above is open and you are ready to receive.

Eight

Eight is not just a number; it is a symbol representing infinity or eternity that transcends any singular lifetime; therefore, it's a supply of infinite abundance. Eight is an energetic frequency that provides empowerment through inner connection to self and spiritual gifts. In Christianity, eight represents the last of all creations: when mankind accepts the Holy Spirit into their hearts. The Tabernacle was dedicated in an eight-day ceremony. Male children are circumcised on the eighth day after birth. Hanukkah is an eight-day holiday commemorating Jews rising up against their oppressors. This number holds the energy of abundance, strength, power, and determination. Affluence is an opportunity to enjoy life and help others oppressed in some way. The notion of infinity is to seek spiritual perfection, completeness, and purity. It also speaks of the perpetuity of time that started long before you or I were here and will last long after we are gone.

Nine

Nine is an exceptionally wise, spiritual energy holding the culmination of all other numeric energy, or spiritual knowledge. It brings cosmic consciousness and awakening of the higher self to align with all that is, was, and ever will be. What started as a seemingly unquenchable thirst on the quest for a sense of self, soul's purpose, and meaning of life is quenched with this energy. The energy of nine defines a typical length of pregnancy, so as a baby forms physically, it also has time for spiritual transformation as a soul takes physical form. Through solid body/mind/spirt connection we all can embrace a higher calling. Enjoy being, then teach the path to enlightenment. Nine is profound in that it's comprised of three trinities (3 + 3 + 3), which further emphasizes its spiritual significance. The essence of "nineness" seems to be synonymous with "maximum," or with the furthest extent of what's possible. Human beings express this notion when they say things such as, "a cat has nine lives," "being on cloud nine," "dressing to the nines," or "going the whole nine yards."[27]

As Franklin D. Roosevelt said, "Happiness is not in the mere possession of money; it lies in the joy of achievement, in the thrill of creative effort." Nine is the existential essence of taking life to the limit and exhausting every possible effort on your part. As I write this, the Eagles song "Take It to the Limit" is playing in my head. To me, it means never give up, because there is always something else you can do—through effort comes experience, which creates life, your life.

Ten

The universal language of ones and zeros is called binary code and has an infinite number of combinations. Ones and zeros indicate feminine and masculine energetic balance. In ancient times ten represented the universe and the totality of human knowledge, as well as the beginning and the end. From the above definitions, zero represents your pure potentiality while one is the start of your life path—ten starts a cycle, and it is the cycle. The spiritual essence of ten reveals your destiny as written in the stars, or written in the book of life if you are a Christian, and speaks of what is possible for you. In the Book of Genesis, the phrase "God Said" is listed ten times, which is testimony of his great power. The Hebrew word for ten is eser,

---

[27] Numerologist, "So What's The Meaning of the Number 9?!" https://numerologist.com/numerology/meaning-of-the-number-9/.

which is close to the word osher, meaning wealth. Perhaps this is why Christians are supposed to tithe ten percent of their earnings to the church. There are Ten Commandments, and there were ten plagues of Egypt. The tree of life is made from ten interconnected nodes. There are ten attributes that add further dimension to spiritual direction related to the tree of life: forward, backward, up, down, left (feminine), right (masculine), lightness, darkness, good, and evil. You are an expression of creation, complete and perfectly made in divine order. Embrace destiny, conspire with all that is above, be guided by magical forces, and awaken. The gift of awakening is knowing and believing that literally anything is possible. Infinite possibilities is the power and energy of ten.

The divine essence of numbers creates a path for your life. When you are on a spiritual journey, you start with nothing, zero. Your soul (zero) decides to come to earth for a purpose, but there is no form to your life yet. The next progression of life is your birth and identification of self. I am here, I am me, and I am one. You take physical form with the energy of one. As life goes on, you experience many kinds of relationships, from which you create many things. Through some relationships, starting in your early childhood, you may develop false and limiting beliefs that dull your sense of purpose in this world. As you continue on with different life experiences, those false beliefs become reinforced. For this reason, many people stop with the vibrational energy of two—they've become stuck and unsatisfied with life. Sometimes the duality and polarity of two energies creates conflict that you are unable to balance, which leads to living a linear life. In essence, you've lost the energy of number one; you've lost yourself. What most people call a mid-life crisis is people unknowingly trying to access the energy of number three. If all you do is purchase a shiny red sports car, then you missed the opportunity to allow your energy to freely flow. Accessing the energy of three helps you tap into positivity and brings your awareness back to self.

By accepting that it's okay to just be, you are embracing the spiritual energy of the number four and creating space inside you that can fill with divine energy. You can tap into this energy through activities such as meditation, breathwork, and sound healing. You need to expel any false beliefs and doubt of self to love yourself fully. This energy helps to create a consistent flow of energy within you, which allows you access the energetic network. The energy of four is feminine, and the energy of five is masculine. Once you're connected to self, Source, and earth with a full cup of energy, then you can authentically do physical things in the world and continue doing things in a spiritual sense, such as connecting to nature. But, you are also connecting to the energy of all that is (divine energy of six) and can then experience synchronicities (divine energy of seven). The more in sync your energy becomes with all that is, the more you notice messages from the other side start to flow. You see and experience patterns that have special meaning to you. You embrace the divine energy of eight when you want more and start to materialize your spiritual gifts—you spend your time wisely.

The lucky people experience the energy of nine as they engage in the journey toward enlightenment. To be enlightened and experience expansion of consciousness doesn't mean you know everything. It is impossible for the human brain to conceptualize how big the energetic network actually is. But, by striving for this knowledge, exerting all effort, you access the energy of ten. You embody your own creation and soul purpose, and therefore, collaboratively work within the energetic network to make things happen. You become magnetic, a master manifestor. As you look upon the stars and the moon, you instinctually know that anything is possible, so you take it to the limit.

7

INTEGRATING ENERGY WORK

Before Engaging Energy

Balance is the key to everything. The Sun and moon balance our days. Gaia needed the universe to balance her energy the way the earth needs water, and fire needs air. The many cycles of nature create balance. To engage in energy work is to create a balanced energetic state in your body, or at least work toward it. In a healthy, high-vibrational, balanced state, how you choose to use your energy is your expression of free-will. You are typically happy and take accountability for all of your actions, thoughts, and words. It doesn't matter who is looking or who isn't; you always act in a way that is authentic to your nature. In an unhealthy, low-vibrational, and unbalanced state, your decisions and behaviors are dependent on your false and limiting belief system—things you believe to be true that are untrue. You lack responsibility and accountability for your actions; therefore, you blame others for the state of your life. When you intentionally use energy, your energy's vibration will rise. Taking purposeful action is automatically responsible and accountable. The fastest ways to grow your spiritual energy are to express kindness and compassion toward yourself and others and express gratitude for all the things in your life.

We've talked about our emotional, mental, physical, and spiritual bodies, but you can also view these as qualities of spiritual energy. Your physical body (the element of earth) measures the quantity of your energy. Your emotional body (the element of water) embodies the quality of your energy. Your mental fortitude (the element of fire) expresses how you focus your energy. And your spiritual essence (the element of air) is the force of your energy. All parts of your being feed off one another to create balance. You may have noticed balance is one of the overreaching themes in this book. If any part of you is over or under stressed by an energetic leak or leaks, then your performance in life suffers because you are imbalanced. If your false and limiting belief system causes you to be unkind to your body, then the other parts of your being cannot work at full capacity. In this example of being unkind to your body, the element of earth can help you find balance again. Maybe you've been studying for months to become a lawyer or CPA and your mental fortitude is shot; use the element of fire to light your spark again, put some passion into your studies, and find balance.

The most elemental aspect to your energy is physical, and the most significant is spiritual, as it influences all the other components. You only have one physical body that you will live in until your body can't go on living anymore. The better you treat yourself, the better quality your life will have, and the longer you have to work toward your life's purpose. Your emotional body is expressed by either positive or negative feelings and directly affects the vibrational level of your energy. When you are emotionally balanced, you automatically treat your body better by choosing high-vibrational foods, moving your body, and implementing good sleep habits. When your focus is in the present moment, you cannot mentally slip off into the past or the future to dredge up feelings of shame, guilt, anxiety, or worry. If you are not present and do not deal with your current undesirable emotions, they will store in your body and wreak havoc in all areas of your life. When you use energy purposefully to engage a spiritual path, you become an energetic force.

Before engaging in energy work and tracking your progress to lunar cycles, you should identify your personal and professional vision. Ask yourself, "What do I want to create?" or "What is my purpose?" Don't think; just start making a list of whatever comes to mind. Then list out your performance barriers and their energetic consequences by asking, "What is in the way of me living authentically?" And please know that you are always allowed to ask, "What do I want?" This information can help you create monthly action plans to track your progress that work with lunar energy to improve your performance. Common energetic leaks in your life could be that you are indecisive, defensive, lack passion or empathy, are overly dependent, moody, or pessimistic, have poor communication skills (to include listening), are too critical of others, or have a negative attitude. It could be a physical issue with your body or an addiction. Most people hear the word addiction and automatically think of drugs or alcohol. You can be addicted to perfection, porn, video games, or bingeing on television. If you are having trouble reaching your goal, really examine how you are spending your time. It's hard to look at yourself in this way, but necessary. Use the energy described in this book to discover more about yourself, your characteristics, and values to help you overcome and decide on what actions to take each month. If the descriptions of certain qualities are something you don't innately possess, then tap into an energetic source with those qualities to help you.

Some of the deepest values you need to improve in your life are health (physically and mentally), faith, responsibility, courage, respect for others, perseverance, friendships, relationships, commitment, creativity, accountability, and, most importantly, authenticity. One of my very first ah-ha moments from when I started my healing journey was that I was mistaking artistic ability with creativity. Once I made that distinction, my creative center blew open. Through your creative nature, you will discover some of the best ways you can use your energy to influence those around you and leave a positive energetic footprint on this earth.

Spiritual Integration

It's the path to oneness and the truth of being which is always greater than the narrowness of the ego mind. As you learn, discover, and gain insight, you have to integrate in order to understand. If you are reading this book, then you are on a spiritual journey, and spiritual integration is the process of living what you've learned. You can't remain in a perpetual state of learning, because that is a type of energetic leak, better known as procrastination. To have deep thoughts is one thing, but integration is about embodiment. It's when you stop living from your head and start leading from your heart. When you self-actualize, you energetically complete a cycle of learning and create space for deeper discovery. Spiritual integration may feel intimidating, but it doesn't have to be complex (remember, your mind adds complexity to your situation). It's an organic process that will naturally occur if you follow Wild Moon Healing principles, starting with strong intention, conducting Moon work, and creating a daily practice with a clear purpose. It could materialize as a balanced vibration, in touch with both your feminine and masculine energies, having the ability to actually let go of that which no longer serves you, or expressing compassion to the world.

Integration is crucial to spiritual awakening and awakening your true, authentic nature. In regard to shadow work and releasing what no longer serves you, you will want to incorporate activities that work with your inner child and future self. When you do, know that the energy from your inner child is about what you need. This is a root necessity, such as love. Learn when your inner child is having a temper tantrum by examining your thoughts and actions. The energy of your future self is about what you want. Understand you have the full capacity to achieve your dreams. No matter where you are in life, you have access to pure potentiality, where anything is possible.

Nervous System

The nervous system guides almost all that you do, think, say, or feel. The name of the game with Wild Moon Healing is to heal. There's a fun word called neuroplasticity, which describes how all of your life experiences make pathways in the brain, affecting all that you do, think, say, or feel, and your brain's capacity to change. You have life experiences that make you, for example, eat too much, drink to excess, procrastinate, or have obsessive or compulsive patterns. These behaviors were created because something was too painful to deal with, so you leaned on alcohol as a support buddy instead of healing. You have the ability to eradicate these patterns energetically, and forever.

My favorite activities to move energy involve integrating movement, meditation, sound, and breath into my rituals. If you decide to implement these practices, they will help you change your neuropathways. Movement should be slow and purposeful and incorporate specific static and dynamic postures to influence your energy. Going to the gym to work out on stationary equipment to become stronger or using the treadmill to improve your endurance running will move your energy but not in the same way. Any type of meditation or prayer opens you up to your Source and higher self, which has strong energetic influences on your regular actions, especially if you practice this daily. Sound healing works to affect your personal vibration through different instruments, such as a crystal singing bowl, rain drum, flute, or a gong. The human body is mainly made up of water, which is greatly affected by the vibration of sound, and these vibrations can bring healing by calming the nervous system.

In my experience, using the modality of breathwork has had the most profound effect on my nervous system. Throughout your life, everything that you do not release is trapped in your body—literally every fiber in your body retains experiences and feelings from trauma. The ego mind is a powerful tool, but it can be a little obsessive in protecting us. In order to not think about all the things that hurt you, your ego mind consciously helps you establish negative behavior patterns to facilitate avoidance. That's its job, to protect you; only it does its job extremely and unreasonably well. These negative behavioral patterns involve inputs through your senses to keep trauma down. Inputs such as eating your feelings, drinking to blackout so you can't see the status of your life, watching porn and wondering why you can't get close to anyone, or using excessive television or gaming to defer your pain. When these patterns turn into addiction, you become stuck in these behaviors and your life is affected in every way imaginable—you gain weight, you can't experience intimacy, you have sleep issues, or your body creates dis-ease to deal with the toxicity you provide it with. By engaging with somatic healing such as breathwork, you get out of your head and back into your body where the issues lay dormant. You can move stuck emotions using breath, which allows you to release them. This isn't like practicing a box breath when you are anxious, or yoga Nidra to slow your mind down before bedtime. Look for a certified breathwork practitioner that is trauma informed to guide you through the process.

Somatic Healing

Somatics describes any practice focused on the connection of mind and body to help you listen to and decipher your internal self and listen to messages from your body such as pain, discomfort, or imbalance. Sounds like a fancy word for Moon work! Somatic therapy is body-centric, focusing first on sensations in your body through modalities such as deep relaxation exercises, mindfulness, and body movement. There are many healing modalities that you can practice that will allow you to access more information about the ways your body stores experiences.

The nervous system stores unresolved trauma in your muscles, tendons, and fascia. This negative energy creates dis-ease in your body. This can lead to problems such as muscle tension, digestive issues, trouble sleeping, or chronic pain. You don't need a psychology degree to help yourself purposely connect with your inner self to discover what you really need in this moment. Your nervous system guides almost everything you do, think, say, or feel. It controls complicated processes like movement, thought, and memory. Through your energy work you will organically begin to heal yourself somatically. In Moon work, you are going after your goals but also learning about yourself and healing. Working with energy will help you work through repressed or blocked emotions related to a traumatic experience. If you engage in healing modalities, such as meditation or purposeful movement like Qigong, you will begin to experience pain relief, move easier, and feel a lighter, more positive energy within.

Nothing in this book replaces anything prescribed by your doctor, including talk therapy or supplementation; however, it enhances it. Moon work is you taking responsibility for the status of your life and your body and expressing accountability by taking an active role in creating change. It all begins with a simple intention.

Creating Intentions

The power of intention is everything in energy work. There is no limit to what you can and cannot ask for, so long as you are not sending out ill will to another, as that will come back to you threefold. Also, you cannot protect yourself against or from something inevitable, like a premature death. Outside of those parameters, if you can imagine it, then you can ask for it. Intentions start the manifestation process. You cannot create an intention and then simply wait for it to happen. That's why during the waxing lunar phase you exert physical energy to work toward your intention. What the universe does is bring opportunity and resources your way to help you accomplish or overcome and ultimately achieve. You still need to act on any divine prospect or contribution when it arrives. As with my experience, any divine intervention or gift is fleeting.

When first creating an intention, don't worry about your words or writing it down; in fact, use as few human words as possible. Instead focus on the essence of your desire and how it makes you feel. Visualize it as if you are watching an old movie of your life because it's already happened (makes it real) instead of the act of reading a book (makes it fiction). Feel emotions well up as you remember. It's a weird concept to remember your future, but it's an excellent resource when you become comfortable with it. The reason you want to feel the emotions is that the universe reacts to your vibration, because words do not exist in the metaphysical universe. The universal law is that like attracts like, so stay in your visualization until you really feel the emotion that you want to create.

Keep it positive. Any negativity such as "can't," "don't," "won't," or even "no" will only attract you more of what you don't want. For example, let's say your intention is that you want to keep your job. If you focus on your intention with the following words, "I don't want to lose my job. My boss can't outsource my position," the energy received by the universe removes all the negative jargon. So, the message received is actually, "I want to lose my job. My boss outsource my position." It isn't grammatically correct, as the universe will not change the energy from "can't" to "will." As you can see, the unintended consequence of a negative mindset will only attract more negativity. Instead, your intention should clearly articulate what you do want. Keeping with the above example, "I want to keep my job for the foreseeable future. My boss will keep all positions in-house and maintain the current benefits I enjoy." Now this intention will attract what you truly desire.

Adding crystals, herbs, and such to your energy work amplifies it because things such as crystals vibrate at a frequency that is naturally much higher than that of most human experiences, because they are gifts from the earth. These aids are metaphysically unable to lower your vibration or create disharmony in your life. What these things can do is expand your energy to vibrate at a higher frequency, such as amplification of positive emotions, manifest greater opportunity, provide protection from harm, and help you fall into alignment with your destiny.

Using Energy

We've discussed many types of energy in this book, so how do you access and use them? The most important thing is to use intention in all that you do. To create change in your life, you have to do something different, start something new, or stop doing something altogether. This encompasses habits, behaviors, and thought processes. If you attempt to invoke the energy of air because you're tired to help shake you into alertness, it may not work as you want if your lifestyle and current life experience don't allow for enough rest. Energy work encompasses physical, mental, and emotional interaction within yourself in order to connect with any energy that is above or below. In the case of exhaustion, you must create change in your life to allow for more restful sleep, while working with the energy of air. If creating time for more quality sleep isn't possible, then you may be calling in the wrong energy. However, if you find yourself bored and want to shake things up a bit, the energy of air can help spark an exciting new idea.

To connect with your chosen energy, first find a quiet and comfortable place where you feel safe to close your eyes and go within. This step seems simple, but it is important and it will make an enormous difference if you know you won't be disturbed. While in this safe place, you will want to take time to breathe and relax so you can shift your awareness from your busy day and environment to being aware of your inner self and the energy you want to work with or create within yourself. Deeply breathing and relaxing, call in your energetic source, spirit guide(s), and higher self to help guide you. Spirit energy comes from another dimension, in the subtle energy realm, so receiving its wisdom and insight is much different from any learning you can do in your physical environment. This is a time of sinking into faith to bring forth the energy of love, kindness, and light. You must be open to the process because if you believe in nothing, nothing will happen.

The consequence of lack of trust or faith can be significant and can affect your healing process. Trust is the foundation of every relationship, including the one you have with yourself, and the source from which your strength grows. Faith is a relationship with something greater than yourself; it is your strength. What I write is about invoking guidance, rather than channeling spirits. Channeling is the practice of a person's body being taken over by a spirit for the purpose of communication. Invocation requires faith as you call guides into your energetic space, knowing they will help you. Raising your vibration takes an element of belief that you can harness different types of energy and use them for the highest good. By taking the time to relax and meditate, you raise your vibration, allowing you to access this energy and empower the process.

Once in a relaxed state, call forth and invoke your spirit guides and source that create your team of powerful support. Any highly evolved spiritual being who is worthwhile in connecting with will honor your free will and will not intervene in your life without your explicit permission. The combination of your consent and intention is what authorizes your connection with your spiritual support team and encourages seeking their presence during your energy work. There is nothing wrong with conversing or seeking favor, but ultimately the goal must always be to elevate your awareness to that of love and wisdom through spiritual masters and seek their purpose. The human experience tends to be one of self-reliance, independence, entitlement, and self-affirmation, so you must surrender and recognize a higher power's ability to repair, strengthen, and guide you. This process is about reverence, to outwardly demonstrate your complete honor and respect for their wisdom. To invoke and call forth your spirit team, you can sincerely, from your heart center, request the connection by saying, "I now call in my team of spiritual masters (this is God, universe, a specific goddess power, etc.) of the highest most benevolent light energy. Please connect with me now and help me experience your energy, love, and wisdom, according to divine will for my benefit. And so it is."

I prayed a similar invocation one time when I needed my brother, David. When you talk to God, the universe, or angels, the answer can come so softly that you miss it because of the demanding lifestyles people live today. In order to reach my brother, a fallen Marine, I had to knock on the door to Valhalla. His response suitably came down loud and proud. My son, who is named after my brother and resembles his name sake in appearance and attitude, enlisted in the Marine Corp. I needed to know that my brother would go with him, protect him, and comfort him. And, if the worst imaginable situation happened, I needed to know that he was there to take my son home. As I paced at my brother's gravesite with my arms flailing about, I said, "I don't know what kind of paperwork is involved, but you need to get it started." Although I'm quite certain there is no paperwork in the spiritual world, I was comprehending things how I know and understand them here on Earth. His response came about ten days later... I recall it was a Thursday. I came home from work, and my son was waiting for me at the kitchen table. He told me his leave date changed and he was now heading to Paris Island about four months early. My brother has helped me and communicated with me in various ways over the years, albeit energetically, and this time was no different. My son's leave date had changed to the 25th anniversary of my brother's death—the boldest case of synchronicity I've ever experienced.

My brother wasn't finished; he wanted to make sure I understood that he was going to comply with all the demands I made of him. I know this because my brother was killed just before the intersection where you turn onto base. Because traffic was bad the day I saw my son off, I sat at that same intersection through three lights. My heart sank, and I couldn't breathe as my mind drifted back twenty-five years. It was a bitter-sweet day while I stayed in silent remembrance of my brother and shared the irresistible excitement with my son, all at the same time. All of those who have gone before us are still here, albeit not in the way we would like, and you can use energy to correspond with them.

Moving your awareness takes practice. If you don't feel like you are really connecting, then learn through repetition—practice makes perfect. Your energy centers may be closed off or sluggish. Practicing Wild Moon Healing principles will open your energy centers. Purposefully engaging the healing process to include shadow work and consistently following lunar cycles and engaging in astrological energy will open you up to this process, as well as open up your internal energy system. The main chakras to work on and strengthen to experience the highest connection is your sacral (creation) chakra, your heart center, and your pineal gland (or third eye). So, as you mediate, start with a focus on your sacral chakra, move to your heart, and then your third eye. See them opening, expanding, and becoming receptive to the energy of your energetic team. Then move your awareness up through your crown chakra and ascend up a pillar of white radiant divine light where you will connect with your guardian angel and divine guide, or spiritual team. Go farther up to unite with Source, God, and divine, all that is. Bask in the light and frequency of its presence.

After this visualization, all you need is to allow the energy to work within you so you can receive messages and transmissions. As you come back into awareness, finish with gratitude. Bring your hands over your heart center and take just a moment to be thankful for whomever showed up for you today and their guidance, support, wisdom, and love. Ask that they continue to guide you and help direct your energy for the highest good. As you begin to journal and track your progress with your energy work, continue to stay aware of how your personal energy has changed, as it is now vibrating at a higher frequency. You will start noticing at once how the energy of things or from a person affect you differently. Believe that your guides and Source are always with you, and as you go about your daily life, you will become more aware of earth and animal energy, and you will start to see more repeating patterns and synchronicities. You will notice that you live more from your heart center rather than your head. You will learn more about yourself and will fall completely in love with you who are, and ultimately will find the path toward your purpose.

Energetic Rhythm

Self-discovery is an intimate, personal journey for everyone. Each phase of the lunar cycle is an opportunity to explore and discover more about yourself from different perspectives. It is as if the phases of the moon exist to create an intelligent, straightforward road map for manifestation. New moon energy can help you discover what you want and how to plant figurative seeds in your life so you can grow and transform. The energy from the waxing moon phase helps you cultivate that which you planted at the new moon and learn about yourself by exploring how you react to people, places, and things. Full moon energy helps you harvest that which you've been working on by exploring your shadows and inner child, the parts of you that you've been protecting from the outside world. Figuratively, the full moon sheds light on your path to help you see things you couldn't see before that you need to eliminate from your life so you can make room for better things. The energy during the waning moon phase helps you prepare the symbolic ground for more seeds as you cultivate forgiveness and love for self. Tuning into the phases of the moon provides you with a structured approach to help you take consistent action toward achieving your goals and awakening your truth so you can create your best life.

The moon represents powerful divine feminine energy, giving life to matters of new beginnings (new moon), transformation (waxing phase), renewal (full moon), and release (waning phase) to create balance. In time, you will find your perfect rhythm and movement that reflect your authenticity in tandem with the moon's energy. When the powerful forces of a vivid intention and inspired action align, their combined energy radiates at a high frequency, and the universe conspires in your favor. An energetic ripple does not stop. It is not bound by time or space. Believe that your actions today are creating a better tomorrow for you, your family, your community… and the world. A little faith can take down a lot of fear.

Energetic influences are cyclical. You see it in the seasons, the way the energy flows through the zodiac one sign at a time, and the way the Sun and moon orbit the Earth. The Roman poet Juvenal said, "Never does nature say one thing and wisdom another." A spiritual awakening is a deep connection with divine energy and profound understanding of the nature of life that creates inner growth and transformation. Spiritual awakening can also be seen as a journey of self-discovery, or as I like to call it, Wild Moon Healing, which is an opportunity to gain insight into your spiritual truths—becoming authentic through profound shifts in consciousness. It's a life-changing cycle, signifying the rhythm of life within. A karmic cycle is a repetitious pattern of events, emotions, or realizations that occur in your life to help facilitate growth. While working with these energetic cycles, you can see how spirituality plays a greater role in influencing psychological well-being.

The moon goddess is an active presence in our healing and transformation journey. Moon energy honors the maiden, mother, and crone. The triple moon goddess reminds us of the cycle of life, growth, death, and rebirth. The triple goddess is a triunity of three distinct aspects united into one being, as you are now every age you've ever been, experience you've ever had, and feeling you've ever felt. It is a symbol of the connection between the physical and spiritual world. Tapping into this energy can help you when you are depressed, want to give up, need a new perspective, or need direction when you are stuck. It achieves this by reminding us of the importance of balance and harmony in all aspects of our being.

Embrace the process and change your life. If you often feel tired or sluggish, chances are it is not because of your busy day or lifestyle; it's because you are not living in alignment with your truth and doing too little of what ignites the light within you. Allow the process of accessing this energetic network to enliven you. Engage in a daily practice that is graceful and respectful of the beautiful person you are. Know there will be special days, such as that of the full moon, where you will change things up a bit. Love the Earth, as she supports your life. Form a relationship with your source and guides and work with your personal energy system.

Working with Chakras

The main thing to remember when working with your personal energetic network is to pay attention to how you treat yourself and others. Some simplistic things, when used with specific intention, can help you influence how you direct your energy, such as eating foods or wearing clothes in the color of the chakra of which you are working. You can use carefully curated affirmations. "I am" statements speak to your root chakra, "I feel" statements reflect the energetic flow of your sacral chakra, "I do" statements speak to the powerhouse in your belly, "I love" statements speak to the strength of your heart chakra, "I speak" statements reflect the energetic flow of your throat chakra, "I see" statements speak to your connection to your inner wisdom, and "I understand" statements reflect how connected you are to your Source.

But, where the rubber hits the road, as they say, is simply taking the time to relax so you can start to balance your energy organically. Figure out ways to slow the rush of life that we all experience. Doing yoga is a fantastic way to balance your chakras and, with a little research, you will find that there are yoga poses that help with each energetic center. For example, mountain pose helps with your root chakra, as it is the basis for all other poses, just like the root chakra is your foundation. It is specific to the lower part of the body, and it's about standing tall and connecting through your feet to the ground that stabilizes you. Considering the way your energy is connected through your energetic network, the mountain pose begins the alignment necessary to start moving your energy. Working with chakras should be fun, but the most important aspect of working with any type of energy is intention.

Meditation and Movement

The mind-body connection requires both stillness and movement to properly hear cues from within and engage in somatic healing. Meditation is one way to still your mind to hear the cues, but you need to make sure your energy is moving. To move your energy, you need to move your body. Have you ever seen someone that was enraged, yelling, with their arms flailing around, making them look like a windsock outside a gas station? They don't even know it, which is what I love about it, but their body knows it has to move that negative energy to get through it... That's why they thrash their arms about. Do you work with someone who paces constantly while talking on their phone due to a demanding job? That pacing helps them move through the energy of stress. Movement affects your energy, which is your physical and spiritual potential energy. If you do not move, your energy will become deficient. Inactive lifestyles cause chronic illnesses and even sleep issues that can keep you in an immobile state. Like attracts like, so physical movement attracts and promotes energetic flow.

Some of the best physical activities to manifest with the moon are yoga and Qigong. The practice of moving into stillness allows you to experience the truth of who you are, create awareness of your physical body, and become more balanced and centered. These purposeful, slow movements can decrease your blood pressure and resting heart rate, decrease pain, and increase your immune system function. You can even meditate while the body is in motion by being mindful and noticing what is going on in your body while performing a task. I'm sure people who say they absolutely cannot meditate still like a nice hot shower. You can turn that steamy experience into a meditative shower by adding a visualization. To energetically use this practice, visualize the water carrying all your worries and burdens away, and watch them go down the drain.

The purpose of meditation is not to stop your thoughts but to bring a sense of calm to your body. As things arise when you are meditating, just acknowledge your thoughts. Let them flow as they come and go, and then return to your breath. Meditation can also improve your intention-creating process. The best way to discover what you know, what you want to do, and figure out who you want to be is to engage in stillness. Through Wild Moon Healing, my theory is that through stillness or meditation, you will acknowledge, control, and choose your feelings, thus creating a healthier you. Acknowledge what is and honor it. Control the feeling, or how you express it, by showing yourself grace. Choose how you want to feel through a visual meditation and bring that feeling back with you into the present moment. Consistently creating stillness in your life is necessary for learning how to listen to your body and discern its messages. Slow down. Pay attention to your body so you can hear its messages.

Tangible Tools

Certain tools can help you with your Moon work and spiritual practice. For example, tools used in yoga could be your mat, a strap, and yoga blocks as you work toward becoming more flexible. If you are working toward a daily meditation practice, you can use mala beads. If you are new to meditation and you know you won't do it daily, and certainly not for thirty or sixty minutes in one sitting, start moving the mala beads through your fingers with each inhale and exhale. Then progress to deepening your inhale and lengthening your exhalation so you move the beads a little slower through your figures. Next time, graduate to moving one bead per complete breath (inhale and exhale). Then deepen your breath again until you hit your thirty- or sixty-minute goal. My latest awesome find is a LoveTuner that I purchased from a social media ad. I love combining meditation with breath and sound, and this little whistle-esque gadget does just that, only the sound is coming from within, created by your own exhale.

There are tangible tools that work with your energy, such as tarot or oracle cards, crystals, incense, pendulums, and dowsing rods. These are divination tools that you can actually touch to give that particular item access to your energy, thereby making its energy available to you. When using cards and pendulums, make an inquiry and then interpret what you see on the card, or notice the force displayed in the moving pendulum or rod. The other tangible item is human touch, knowing that all that you let into your energetic field will either take your energy or help raise your energetic vibration. If you are lucky enough to come home to a faithful furry companion, then you know what I mean here. Areas with more receptors are found in places that humans use to explore, such as your hands and feet. The receptors or other chakra energy centers allow for energetic transactions with your environment. Practicing earthing transfers the earth's electrons into you, but you can also let Gaia absorb and recycle your negative emotions, trauma, illness, or whatever ails you.

Think about the elements for a moment. Water flows, earth grows, air blows, and fire bellows... These adjectives describe movement of living energy that you can interact with, that also has the potential of drastically restoring or depleting your personal energy reserves. In general, water is cleansing in nature and is used for many purposes in rituals. But a hot shower can slow your energy and prepare you for restful sleep, while a cold shower can wake you up in the morning to prepare you for a busy day. A light breeze on a sweltering day can feel wonderful, so you stop and take it all in, but a long car ride in a convertible with the top down may leave you feeling tired. As with the saying, "You have to feel it to heal it," if you can feel it, then there is an energetic exchange. This includes things you can *feel energetically*, like if someone says something and it makes your skin crawl, or immediately puts a smile on your face.

Hand Energy

The human hand contains a lot of information and energy. You have two hands representing yin and yang energy, serving as conduits to give and receive. When you meet someone, it's customary to extend your arm and shake hands. Between a handshake and eye contact, much energy is exchanged. If you fall, given the opportunity, you will most likely put your hands out in an effort to protect yourself. Some people have the reaction to extend their arm out to their right with their palm facing backwards or down if they have to hit their breaks or experience a sudden stop while driving in effort to protect someone else. Certain emotions cause us to cross our arms and hide the palms of our hands because, even if we aren't consciously aware of it, we instinctually know to protect our hand energy. Through palm chakras you can heal yourself and others, scan auras, send and receive energy, and balance your spiritual, emotional, and mental bodies. Also, using the sense of touch can enhance your creativity and help you feel the vibration in things, such as crystals. Your hands are not only energy centers; physical features of the hands can interpret personality characteristics and predict your future. Learning how to use and interpret your hands is a powerful and magical tool.

Your hands can radiate energy stemming from your heart chakra down through your shoulders and arms to help you manifest what your heart desires. The saying *bless your heart* can hold a negative connotation in the nicest possible way, but also when you truly feel blessed, you may cup your hands and draw them to your chest. When you do this, you are actually helping the energy infuse with your heart center. If you hear something disturbing, you may automatically put your crossed hands over your heart, which is how you instinctually protect your heart energy. Be mindful of who you touch and let touch you because energy transfer is real. Human touch can be amazing or paralyzing. You can direct personal energy in your body by using your hands to touch parts of yourself that hurt to heal or parts of you that crave to satisfy. I am a Reiki practitioner and use my hands to perform a transfer of universal energy that helps to promote relaxation, stress reduction, and symptom relief, improving overall health and well-being. It seems to magically help put people in a meditative state without actually touching them.

Being in conflict with what you are giving or receiving (i.e., your heart isn't in it) can cause your hand energy to become blocked. A blocked hand chakra may express through numbness or tingles in your hand or fingers, or other problems with your hand, wrist, arm, or shoulder. When someone says, "I have the weight of the world on my shoulders," that is an energetic block. Sometimes the best thing you can do to experience instant relief is talking about your worries, asking for help, and even acknowledging that you don't need to carry this particular burden; use hand energy to just put it down. Many people find it easy to give but so hard to receive or even ask for help, because they have a false and limiting belief that they don't deserve to receive love or healing touch, which can block the healing energy in their hands.

Specific fingers and hand positions represent one of your main seven energy centers. Starting with the pinky finger, which represents the heart chakra, the next finger represents the third eye, the middle finger represents the solar plexus, your pointer finger represents the throat chakra, the thumb represents the sacral chakra, the palm of the hand represents the crown chakra, and the wrist represents the root chakra. If you think about it, the solar plexus is your powerhouse, and many people use the middle finger to strongly express their feelings. If you are in a heated conversation and start to shake your pointer finger and shout, it could indicate that you do not feel heard, have issues verbally expressing your truth, or are unable to create healthy boundaries. When people feel blessed or moved by Source, they extend their arms up above their head with palms facing upward to help them connect to the divine. Some people hook their pinky fingers together to indicate a heart bond. Considering body language and use of hands as expression, the chakra placements make sense.

Palmistry is the practice of reading the lines on your palms as a divination tool to tell you more about your character, or to foretell future life events. Take a picture or a Xerox of your palms because the lines change over your lifetime. In life we have free will, and therefore, the lines on your palms must change to reflect your choices in life. A child's palm doesn't have many lines compared to the complexities of an adult's hand because they have just begun to live and make life decisions. Start by looking at your hands and noting what you see. Do you have rough palms or manicured hands? Nothing should be overlooked with divination practices; everything has meaning. Use your intuition and you'll seamlessly extract the meaning of the smallest details. Information relating to chakras, planets, and the zodiac are contained in your fingers. The folds and creases of the palms, referred to as lines, are used to form narratives and predict future happenings. Reading palms and hands can even include messages from fingernails and arms. Different shapes of hands represent the four elements providing more information about your character. For instance, I am a Libra (air sign) and I have square hands, which represent earth and explain my practicality in most matters. As a Libra I am supposed to enjoy the finer things in life, but in reality, I love to get dirty. In the words of Eartha Kitt, "I trust the dirt. I don't trust diamonds and gold." Learn to read the lines and mounts on your hands, as they contain a wealth of knowledge.

While reading palms is a science to be learned, like tarot, working with the energy from your palm chakra can be personal and imaginative. The hands of yogis and those that meditate take unique forms as hand gestures called mudras. You can invoke the power of your hands to evoke a particular state of mind and change your mood, attitude, or perspective. A mudra is an energetic seal that locks energy in the body related to a particular symbol or sacred hand position. This internalization of energy improves the mind-body connection to keep you focused, while helping to heal physical and mental health conditions. Although you may not be aware of the Gyan mudra,[28] commonly known as the gesture of knowledge, learning, and wisdom, you may do it from time to time without knowledge of its significance. This mudra is done by bringing the tip of your index finger and thumb in contact, while extending the other three fingers out straight. This hand gesture joins the elements of fire and air needed to build and grow your knowledge by sharpening your brain, improving concentration, and relieving stress and anxiety.

The best use of hand energy is to create goodness for yourself and others. If something goes hand and hand with something else, it's because they're so closely related that they just inherently go together or happen concurrently. Examples are grit and determination, health and happiness, or honesty and recovery. These idioms indicate unity and the necessity to create and enhance your wellbeing. Creativity is a powerful tool, so use your hands to transform your inner energy to produce something tangible for positive mental health. Anyone with a troubling story, including the loss of limbs or hands, possesses authentic inventiveness to turn raw emotions into refined culture. You are not excluded by any means through any disability. Creative action through hand energy can turn undermining forces that seek to upset your energetic balance into usable energies.

Be Good to Your Body

I wish I treated my body better over the years. Know that it's never too late to start doing so. You can work with energy all day long, but if you continue to treat your body badly, your energy will vibrate at a low frequency. As they say, "Garbage in, garbage out." If you want to raise your energetic vibration, then be good

---

[28] Susan Williams, "What Is Gyan Mudra? 10 Benefits of the Yogic Hand Gesture for Peace," https://yogapractice.com/yoga/gyan-mudra/.

to yourself. I am not only alluding to diet, movement, stillness, and supplementation. Examine all the inputs in your life. That is everything you take in through all your senses—from food, music, and time spent watching television or porn, to reading and learning. Are you spending your time in a manner that would make your body happy? Something you may not think about is breathing. We breathe all day long, but you may not be aware of what you are breathing in, as molecules can't be seen, so keep your environment as clean as possible. If you need medical help, please seek it, but here I am writing about everything within your control, like your behaviors and habits.

Activities to engage in to be good to your body include the obvious: drink water, eat healthy, and move. But also, declutter, minimize sedentary activity, and engage your brain. All the dreams and aspirations you have for life and all the energy and manifestation work you do cannot be realized when you are physically or mentally unhealthy. If you are unhappy at your job, it affects your entire being in an unhealthy way. If you are in an unhealthy relationship, you will never materialize your true self, or be able to show up for yourself authentically. If you binge on television or gaming, you will never realize your potential while you are wasting precious time. All of this is about being good to your body to raise your energetic vibration. Know you can come back from anything, albeit maybe not in the way you predicted.

8

USING ENERGY

Energetic Tools

U sing lunar cycles can help you create the consistent practice of self-care necessary to achieve your goals. The ultimate goal is to create daily practices that honor you and what you are working toward creating in your life. By energetic tool, I mean healing modalities such as meditation or breathwork, but also divination tools. Get all your tools out of the proverbial toolbox and display them so your energy fuses with it—by this I mean create a daily practice. When you create a daily practice and you have an overly stressful day, your meditation or breathing technique will calm you down. Through a daily practice you will notice that things you need in order to help you achieve your goal start to show up for you. You will see signs that you are going in the right direction all over the place. Over time, through following lunar cycles and creating a daily practice that works for you, you will better understand what you can achieve during a lunar cycle, create contingency plans for what derails your progress, and achieve a balanced life by analyzing your daily choices and activities. Opportunities and people will show up to help you expand your experience, challenge you to grow, and help guide you to live authentically.

As a culture, we need to stop using the phrase "tools in a toolbox." If you store away all the things you do and use to raise your energetic vibration, thereby helping you become the healthiest, happiest you that is possible, when you find yourself in crisis and you reach for one of those tools, the effect of its use will most likely not match your expectations. Let's use an example of a tool everyone may own—a flashlight. Everyone has one, but most people don't experience loss of electricity, or need to use their flashlight every day. So, when the lights do go out and you go into your junk drawer, you discover it's not there. Knowing that your flashlight app will soon die since you didn't charge your phone, you run upstairs to the hall closet and... you find a flashlight! Only to discover there are no batteries in it. You know you just saw batteries in the junk drawer so you go back downstairs to find that you have every battery size except for the one you need. But, you found some matches! Now you start looking for a candle, only to remember you stopped burning candles and only diffuse essential oils now. So there you are, sitting in the dark...

This flashlight example is what happens when you engage in a healing modality or use an energetic tool only when things go bad. In the midst of chaos, you can't think straight. A daily practice is just that... practice for when things go awry. The repetition of a daily practice interacting with your personal energy and any of your tools is what helps your "tools" to work properly. My son, David, told me a story about driving into the city to pick up a friend. He was approached by someone he observed to be in an irate state of mind in the middle of rush hour traffic waving around a handgun. Before the individual got back in his car and drove away, he shot my son's tire. It could have been him, not just his tire, but "could have" energy is negative, so don't play that game. The reason I tell you this story is because if I found myself in that situation, I have absolutely no tool to prepare me or keep me calm while my life is being threatened with a gun. But, my son does! He's a United States Marine. He told me, "I don't know how I kept so calm through it all."

I responded, "It's your training." The repetition of drills in boot camp and all his training since prepared him for that chaotic moment in his civilian life.

Your Moon work practice, rituals, divination tools, and healing modality you choose to follow and work with is preparing you for some event in your future. If you use your tools regularly, then on your best days and worst days, you will respond in a similar fashion. Without a normal routine working with energy, you'll react, and a reaction is just fuel for someone else's issue. Whatever that future experience turns out to be, you will handle it with grace under fire. People will ask you how you remained so calm. My son had a friend in the car with him. His friend has never served in the military or received training for a situation like the one they found themselves in. My son's energy helped keep his friend calm too. The more training (i.e., daily practice) you engage in, the more it will not only help you in chaotic situations but also possibly help those around you. Think about the opposite for a moment; we've all been in a situation when our fear or anger grew because someone around us was exhibiting those same emotions. When you don't practice and work toward becoming the person you want to be, it is easy to be pulled into someone else's negative energy. Had my son said or done something that remotely matched the shooter's energy, he probably would have become a fatality that day.

You don't need to follow the same practice all the time; in fact, practicing different modalities on certain days only expands your energetic portfolio. It's okay to only journal on the days you work with new or full moon energy, do a breathwork class once a month, or use different meditations nightly. The takeaway is: creating a daily practice is key to working with energy or energetic tools that will prepare your future self in your future life.

Rituals

The Cambridge dictionary definition of ritual is "a way of doing something in which the same actions are done in the same way every time, or a fixed set of actions and words, especially as part of a religious ceremony."[29] It matters not what words you choose to use—whether it be a ritual, routine, or practice. Speak and use words that make you feel comfortable. The point is that you must do it your way. Design how you work with energy to be as unique as you are and exclusive to your needs, wants, and desires. Some rituals you will do every morning, such as make your coffee and brush your teeth, while your nightly ritual may include reading your Bible, meditating, or working with tarot cards. Some rituals you will only do under the strawberry full moon or only during eclipse season. Rituals are personal and specific to your purpose.

Working with energy via a ritual is about awareness and evaluation. How does that morning coffee make you feel? Do you sleep better when you perform a nightly ritual? Try different things with the intention of being aware of how they make you feel. Maybe try learning a breath technique called *breath of fire* to replace your morning coffee as a test to see if it provides you with the same feeling and benefits as your caffeinated beverage (seriously, I dare you!). With intention, create a crystal grid on your altar for specific purposes, such as better health or to

---

[29] Cambridge University Press, "Meaning of Ritual in English," https://dictionary.cambridge.org/us/dictionary/english/ritual.

attract money and abundance on all levels. Sit with the grid daily and just tune into your feelings—is it working? Nightly work with a tarot deck can combine your energy with this tool and raise your intuition—is it working?

Another key when interacting with energy and creating a ritual is to make sure it's something you want to do and enjoy doing. If you work to set up space and set aside time to start a journaling practice, but you hate journaling, the ritual of a nightly journaling practice may not work out for you. What you create should be in alignment with what you are working on and what you like doing. If all of the information contained in this book is new to you and you have no idea where to start, name one thing that caught your interest and do some research to learn more. We complicate things in our minds, but working with energy isn't complicated. Here are some simple suggestions to get you started:

- If chakras piqued your interest, start by looking up a chakra meditation online, work with it for a week, and see how it influences your behavior and mood. Check in with yourself before you begin and take note of how you feel (literally write this down because you may forget) and reevaluate after a week. It's as simple as that.
- Purposefully go outside and put your bare feet on the natural soil with the intention of exchanging energy with the earth.
- Use pre-established journaling prompts to learn more about yourself. There are many journaling prompts for this purpose in my book *Wild Moon Healing*.
- Find a Reiki practitioner near you and go to a few appointments to see if it helps move your energy and raise your energetic vibration.
- Make moon water by setting a glass container of water outside under the moon. Create an intention over it, and then use it in a manner that matches

your intention. Maybe your intention is for financial growth. Use your moon water to water your plants, and experience positive changes with your finances as your plants grow.

Tarot, Oracle Cards, and Pendulums

Tarot cards, oracle cards, and pendulums are holistic tools that can help you clarify your vision and make sense of things, such as how past influences are affecting your present experience, what is happening in your life, what you should release, and how to best move forward. Use of tarot or oracle cards helps you access your personal energy and tap into your subconscious mind, inner knowing, and higher self. Your energy engages based on the imagery on the cards to access information that's stored in your subconscious mind, enhancing clarity and self-reflection. These metaphysical tools help you connect with your intuitive knowing. Use your knowledge about numerology and colors (see candle magick later in this section) to gain more understanding and help you interpret the meaning of the card. If there is an animal on the card, research it to find its meaning. Remember, your energy flows like a river, changing constantly. So, the messages in the cards will change continually as well.

Oracle decks are excellent guidance tools for self-care rituals and are easier to learn than tarot. Although limited in details compared to tarot, oracle decks supply the "big picture." Tarot is structured in a specific order for a reason, providing detailed personal information or insights, but it also takes time to learn. So, if you are new to card reading, oracle decks are a good place to start. Their guidance can provide you with helpful affirmations and practices to use on your self-healing journey. Use tarot cards if you want a detailed reading and oracle cards for general advice or information. Both can be used to connect with your higher states of consciousness.

It is possible to use a pendulum for guidance on its own or with divination cards. Pendulums help clarify your cards when you ask yes/no questions. There are ways to get more information from a pendulum, such as using a dowsing board. You can create a pendulum by suspending a weighted object from a chain so it is able to swing freely. Think of a pendulum as a simple harmonic oscillator that moves in tandem with your personal energetic vibration. You can use a piece of jewelry, a crystal, or a small household item to make your own pendulum. If you buy a new pendulum, you should cleanse it and program it before using it. To program it, purposefully swing it one direction and say, "This is yes." And then swing the opposite direction and say, "This is no." You can also ask your pendulum prior to each use which way it wants to go for yes or no. You can clear its energy by holding it over sage smoke for a few seconds, laying it in a bed of sea salt overnight, or holding it under running water for a few seconds. If you use water, make sure it is safe to expose the crystal on your pendulum to water. Water has the potential to cleanse—or destroy—your crystals. Do your research so you know how to properly care for your crystals.

Sacred Geometry

Some believe that sacred geometry and numerology are the building blocks of our universe and reality. The power of three, six, and nine is something everyone should research. I always see numeric patterns, even when I'm helping friends decipher their tarot readings. Sacred geometry is like a universal kaleidoscope. It uses an ancient science that explains the core principles of how energy naturally organizes. Sacred geometric patterns are fundamental structures upon which all matter is built. Sacred geometry reveals hidden answers about how your inner and outer worlds can unite to create balance and harmony. Basic geometric shapes of a circle, square, triangle, cross, and spiral have deep meaning.

- Circle – A powerful symbol of oneness, unity, inclusiveness, wholeness, and even perfection. It is the essence of feminine energy, the womb, and continuous flow of energy. The beginning and the end are inseparable. In math you see this calculation in Pi—it goes on forever and never repeats. The creative potential that exists here is amazing, because at its center is a vortex of power. It is where information and ideas circulate, yet nothing is concrete.

- Square – A symbol of practical and solid energy with a grounding characteristic that denotes stability, balance, and dependability. This shape is associated with the number four and the root chakra.

- Triangle – A symbol of balance and harmony (remember earlier when I discussed "fourness" and the perfect triangle?). You can see the power of three in such concepts as mind, body, soul or maiden, mother, crone.

- Cross – Sheer simplicity expressing the connection between Heaven and Earth and the birth of humanity. It is not a coincidence that Jesus was crucified on a cross. Also, the cross is the symbol of the heart chakra, which is your bridge connecting the spiritual chakras to the material and your connection to receive and give love and light.

- Spiral – Also referred to as the Fibonacci sequence or the golden ratio, the spiral can be thought of as a physical manifestation of the expression "as above, so below" and as you evolve through learning and energy work, your consciousness spirals outward, eventually connecting your physical self with your higher self. Mathematically, it starts with two 1's, and every number afterward is the sum of the two previous numbers.[30] You can see this in things from a tiny snail to your DNA, and how energy flows through your chakra system.

The Flower of Life, arguably one of the most well-known examples of sacred geometry, is a beautiful work of art. It's made up of a group of seven overlapping circles that unify in the form of a flower that represents inherent interconnectedness between all living things.

Sacred geometry is not just math and shapes; you see it represented in nature and music too. In music what you are hearing are vibrations, which can indeed be measured mathematically. There is a reason fast tempos get you moving, while slower tempos calm you down. I love attending a soundbath; my friend Kim is so amazing and talented—the vibrations she creates with her instruments can calm you. I've attended her soundbaths at multiple locations. One place she plays used to be an indoor pool, and the acoustics there are amazing—vibrations from the gong are almost orgasmic. I also use sound in my own practice and personal rituals because it's physically and emotionally healing. Alexandre Tannous is an ethnomusicologist, sound therapist, and sound researcher. For the past twenty-two years, he has been researching the therapeutic and esoteric properties of sound from three different perspectives—Western scientific, Eastern philosophical, and shamanic societal beliefs—to gain a deeper understanding of how, and to what extent, sound has been used to affect human consciousness.

You can see and experience sacred geometry on myriad levels, and understanding how it works can be beneficial. As Foster says, "When we exist in accordance with these sacred principles, we are in a state of abundance and receptivity—

---

[30] Jane Kight, "What Is Sacred Geometry? The Ultimate Beginner's Guide." https://www.omniaradiationbalancer.com/blogs/news/sacred-geometry-beginners-guide.

we become energetic architects and empowered co-creators of our reality."[31]

Crystals and Gridding

One of the wonderful aspects of working with metaphysical tools such as numerology, astrology, or crystals is how easy it is to use these tools together, and how they help to amplify each other's energy and your own energy work. Crystal energy works with sacred geometry and numerology.

Before you start gridding, you should learn about and accumulate a personal collection of crystals and stones. The most important concept to be aware of when choosing crystals is that they really choose you. You can sometimes tell if there is a connection by holding it in your hand, closing your eyes and trying to connect with it, and feeling its vibe. Maybe the color of a certain stone catches your eye—it's always for a reason. Trust the universe. If it draws you in, pick it up. Do you feel tingling or a sense of inner peace? These are signs that the stone has chosen you.

Crystals

Beginner Crystals to Explore

- Rose quartz has the ability to clear negative energy from your environment to allow the energy of love, positivity, and forgiveness to enter. You can use it for self-empowerment. This crystal is connected to your heart. It opens you up to the possibilities of goodness and self-love and connects with the throat chakra so you can lovingly speak your truth.

---

[31] Alexandre Tannous, "About Alexandre Tannous," https://soundmeditation.com/about/.

- Hematite promotes self-esteem, boosts confidence, and balances energy to rid you of negativity. It helps you bring your inner "me" energy out into the collective by grounding and protecting you. This stone helps get rid of toxic energy, negative thoughts, and anxiety over past traumas. Hematite is associated with your root chakra, promoting feelings of safety, and your solar plexus, your powerhouse, to allow you to take on whatever life throws at you. This stone also helps balance your yin/yang energy.
- Smokey quartz is great for inner child work, as it rids you of negative thoughts and toxic vibes that no longer serve you. Use this to overcome fears, balance emotions, and stop old negative patterns. This crystal works with your root chakra to help you build a solid foundation by breaking free from self-destructive behaviors and renewing your body and spirit.
- Selenite has incredible cleansing powers and the ability to connect to higher states of consciousness. This can not only clear your environment of negative energy, but it can also help cleanse your other stones after you use them. Use this crystal with the element of fire (e.g., light a candle) to enhance its transformational powers and raise your and your environment's energetic vibration. It is also used to change old thought patterns and how you interpret what you see; therefore, it is associated with the third eye and the crown chakras.
- Moonstone is one of my favorites to help keep you in tune with the natural world and all of its many and varied cycles. This stone is affluent with feminine energy, inner strength, and personal growth. If you need to spark some inner power, moonstone can help balance emotions, sharpen intuition, and strengthen

self-confidence. Use it to bring balance to your heart, crown, and third-eye chakras.

- Labradorite is a stunning stone that appears to magically change color right before your eyes. Some people believe it holds trapped light from the Aurora Borealis. If change stresses you out, get this as a palm stone and keep it on your person at all times—because change is inevitable (I keep one in my purse!). This stone can help rid you of fears and inhibitions by building trust in the universe and promoting faith in yourself. This stone has a strong connection to the spirit world through insight and clarity, so it works well with third-eye and crown chakra work.

- Amethyst is a crystal everyone should own. This stunning purple stone has been used for centuries to create an amazing, meaningful connection to the goodness of the universe. It helps when your energy feels stuck and unable to move forward by clearing your emotional fog. Both the third-eye and crown chakras may benefit from amethyst's healing vibrations.

- Tiger's eye has the potential to raise your vibration when you feel intimidated to bring about the courage, strength, and brave attributes of the tiger animal spirit. Use this stone to help clear out any self-doubt holding you back. Use this stone to work with your powerhouse (solar plexus).

- Black obsidian releases negative dark energies through its protective and healing powers. If you feel like a dark cloud is always hanging over you, use this stone to invoke the powers of the Sun. Due to its protective powers, it is believed that this stone can help you connect to spirit guardians and the angelic realm. Use this stone to work with your crown chakra if you are seeking a higher level of psychic and cosmic connection.

- Clear quartz is often referred to as "the master healer" because of its overabundance of healing qualities. Use this crystal to enhance the power of any other crystal or stone you are working with. It is thought to have the strongest vibration of any crystal. Clear quartz can clear negative energy in you and your environment and give you a burst of energy and motivation. Use this with your crown chakra work to enhance your spiritual potential and gain insight.

Gridding

When you become comfortable working with crystals and stones, you may feel inspired to start gridding. Gridding is the act of laying out stones in a pattern that is recognized in sacred geometry and is amplified by your intention. You can add candles, flowers, or herbs to your grid as well. People grid to channel the essence of the stones' energies into their everyday lives. You can make your own grids, buy a premade grid, or print out a mandala drawing to help you get started. In sacred geometry there are specific designs or patterns that have some sort of spiritual meaning associated with them. Pick a design that either resonates with you or is linked to the intended outcome of your intention.

Once you buy your first stones, you will need to know how to properly cleanse them after each use and prepare them to use in your sacred geometry grid. My favorite way to lay them out is under the energy of a full moon. You can simply run water over them (research your stone to make sure water won't damage it), store them in a container with a salt base, or put them in your house plants to absorb earth energy. When you clear your crystals, make sure you clear your space where you are gridding. You can smudge the room (burn sage) or use incense and crack a window so any negative energy can escape and the energy of air will take it where it needs to go. Then, simply start with your biggest stone in the center and work your way outward from there, constructing your grid by placing stones in even intervals. Incorporate as much symmetry as possible into the grid. As you create your grid, home in on an intention and keep this in mind as you lay the stone. Intention is everything. The simple act of writing out your intention and placing it under your grid can reinforce your intention.

Once you're finished, the grid needs to be activated, so as soon as you complete your grid and have admired your work, really become clear on your intent. In a moment of peace, become incredibly clear on the desired outcome. Close your eyes and visualize your intention as if what you want to create is already in existence. When you are finished, open your eyes and, using your pointer finger on your dominant hand (or a wand if you have one), trace an invisible line connecting all the crystals and stones on your grid. Do this slowly, with your intention in the forefront of your mind. The process of tracing the stones uses your energy and the energy of your intention to connect the crystals and attune them to one another. Keep your grid somewhere convenient, as you may want to retrace it every few days to raise its energetic vibe. Crystals give and receive energy constantly, and as they give, they need to be replenished.

Candle Magick

Candles can be magical, and candle magick can be simple or complex. This is up to you, and there is no right or wrong way to do it—there is only your way! The basic practice is to light a candle and say a prayer. Even if this topic is too woo-woo for you, the gentle act of lighting a candle has a calming effect, as it provides light when you find yourself in the dark. I know from experience that even when the lights go out in a church, it's a scary place. Candles are used in many religions and cultures, and most notably, candles are used as a birthday ritual—you have to blow out the candles on your birthday cake in order to make a wish. If you find yourself curious, but not really sure about candle magick, keep reading...

Fire is a powerful element that represents transformation, and using a candle can invoke the energy of fire. Fire changes everything it interacts with, such as making water boil to destroying the photograph of your ex-lover. Candles are used to amplify and release energy. The candle itself can be used as a decoration (you don't have to light it) with the intention that it provides positive vibes in your environment. But a lit candle channels transformational energy that encourages and accelerates change in your life. The act of burning a candle connects you to the spiritual realm. Different colored candles store distinct types of energy. You can, for example, place a pink candle near your home's doorway invoked with the intention to welcome in love, or keep a yellow candle on your desk with the intention of influencing your career.

Colored Candle Meanings

- Black is used for psychic protection. It represents loss, sadness, releasement, negativity, protection, and banishing.
- Blue connects with your chakras and any emotional wounds that need healing. It represents dreams, sleep protection, spiritual awareness, peace, patience, understanding, and intuition. Use dark blue for depression and vulnerability issues.
- Brown helps with all things relating to your resources (like good health, positive energy, material possessions, pets, and even courage). Sounds like the root chakra to me, so use it for any earth or animal-related work. It represents stability, friendships, and you can even use it for gardening.

- Gold is used for financial gain, business endeavors, and solar connections.
- Green helps bring your ideas to life and amplifies prosperity. It represents fertility, success, healing, prosperity, financial gain, abundance, luck, and harmony.
- Orange encourages your ambition and helps you broaden your horizons. It represents encouragement, attraction, concentration, legal aid, courage, and intellect.
- Pink is for romance and represents friendship, tranquility, love, unity, harmony, beauty, and emotional healing.
- Purple boosts your spiritual enlightenment and creativity. It enhances power and ambition and is used as a healing agent or to reverse a curse.
- Red encourages love, sex, and passion. It represents health, protection, vitality, courage, sexuality, and passion. Passion can also be a powerful desire to create positive change in the world.
- Silver is used for reflection, intuition, and lunar connections!
- White promotes serenity and peace, enhancing personal strength and insight. It represents truth, purity, purification, strength, and cleansing. A white candle can also substitute for any other color—just use intention to indicate the color you need.
- Yellow enhances your persuasion, networking, and social skills, bringing in new career opportunities, and is also associated with material possessions. It represents memory aid, charm, confidence, happiness, protection, and travel.

As with all energy, there are different qualities to candle energy that can further enhance the energy and impact of your efforts. You can use a specific color on a certain day to enrich your goals. So, if you are using candle magick to influence your career, light a yellow candle on Wednesday. Here are the days of the week that will amplify the energy of specific candle colors.

Colors per Days of the Week

- Sunday: gold and orange
- Monday: silver, white, and gray
- Tuesday: red, brown, and other autumn shades
- Wednesday: yellow and gray
- Thursday: purple and deep blue
- Friday: light blue, green, pink, and copper hues
- Saturday: maroon, dark shades, and black

You can use one candle to focus on one thing, or you can mix-n-match, get creative, and use multiple candles of different colors to tackle your desires with more vigor. To start a candle ritual, carefully pick a plain candle in the appropriate color that corresponds with the nature of your goal and try to use it on a specific day to amplify its effects. You may also want to place relevant crystals, herbs, essential oils, or flowers around your candle to amplify the right vibes.

Herb Correspondence

- Ash – protection, health, prosperity, luck
- Basil – protection, love, courage, wealth
- Beet Root – love
- Burdock Root – protection, healing, release negative energies
- Chamomile – improved sleep, purification, luck
- Clover – success, luck, fidelity, protection

- Frankincense – purification, spirituality, success, cleansing
- Ginger – prosperity, love, power, success
- Hyacinth – happiness, protection, love
- Nutmeg – fertility, luck, prosperity, breaking hexes
- Thistle – strengthens energy, healing, protection
- Vervain – increase wealth and love, repels psychic negativity, purification, peace

Make sure any herbs or flowers are finely ground so they stick to the candle with ease. Holding or gazing upon the unlit candle, think of what you want to attract or change in your life and set a clear intention. Be specific, realistic, positive, and kind. You can scribe your candle. Use a ritual knife or pin to carve names, numbers, symbols, or key words associated with your goal into your candle—be creative. Now you can anoint your candle with an appropriate oil or combination of oils, then add herbs or flowers so they stick. Start by putting a few drops of essential oil on your finger and trace around anything that you scribed into the candle. Some popular oils to use in rituals and their associated purpose are as follows:

Oil Correspondence

- Anise – purification, protection
- Bergamot – success, prosperity
- Camphor – banishing illness, psychic awareness, harmony
- Cinnamon – prosperity, astral projection
- Clary Sage – cleansing of negativity and banishing
- Dragon's Blood – love, protection, good luck
- Eucalyptus – purification, healing
- Jasmine – love, prosperity, astral travel, clairvoyance
- Lavender – cleansing, healing, love, tranquility
- Orange – personal power, luck

- Patchouli – personal growth, physical attraction, prosperity
- Sandalwood – personal healing, banishing illness, spirituality, protection

When using oils in a ritual, add a carrier oil like fractionated coconut oil. A base carrier oil serves several purposes. One is to thicken the oil to help secure any herbs or flowers you are using. The second is to avoid any skin irritation if you choose to anoint your person. Also, the cost of oils can be pricey, so adding a carrier oil helps them to last longer.

At this point you will speak aloud the spell or blessing with intention and focus. You can simply state the intention, and read the words you scribed into the candle, or you can get creative and read a poem or sing a song about your intention. The extra effort tells the universe you are committed to your goal. Now light your candle. Gaze into the flame with your focus on your intention. Breathe deeply. You can perform a box breath where you inhale for four counts, hold for four counts, exhale for four counts, hold for four counts, and repeat. Sit in meditation with your thoughts while you visualize your outcome. Stay in meditation until you actually begin to feel as though your goal has been reached. Embrace that feeling so you can bring it back into the present moment with you. Maintain the process until you feel fulfilled and content. Let the candle burn out on its own if it's possible and safe. Do not go to sleep or leave an unattended lit candle in your home. Always use a fire-safe container, and have water nearby just in case.

Just remember that candles invoke the element of fire and channel transformation and change. The basic way to use a candle is to light a candle and say a prayer or your intention—this is a pretty standard spiritual practice and not unfamiliar territory for most people. I encourage you to turn your intention or goal into a poem to enhance the effects. An example for adding more joy to your life would be:

I could use a little more joy today,
If you have some to spare, please send it my way.
More happiness please come to me,
As I will, so mote it be.

If you write your intention or poem on paper, you can fold the paper. Fold the paper toward your body if you want to bring in this energy and fold the paper away from your body if you want to expel a certain energy. Hold the folded paper over the flame to catch fire (without burning your fingers and in a safe environment with a fire-proof bowl). As your intention disappears, know the universe received it and has begun working in your favor.

Chakra Balance Meditation

A straightforward way to use energy is through meditation. This is a chakra meditation. You are going to revitalize your internal energetic network by focusing on each chakra to release stagnant energy, align your energetic body, raise your vibration, and free your authentic self. You may do this in silence, or you may want to play some meditative music of your choice. Start by finding a comfortable position… You can lay down, sit cross legged on the floor, or sit in a chair with your feet flat on the ground. Straighten your spine. Relax your arms. If you are comfortable with closing your eyes, you may do so. They may close naturally as you start taking three deep breaths in and out through your nose. If it's more comfortable, you may breathe through your mouth. As you work on each charka, go as fast or slow as you want through the meditation, but try to take some time with each energy center.

Breathe in positive energy to the count of 3-2-1. With your exhale, release any stagnant energy (3-2-1). Breathe in hope and faith (3-2-1). With your exhale, release any doubt or uncertainty (3-2-1). Breathe in joy and ease (3-2-1). As you exhale, release any stress or unease (3-2-1). Continue breathing deeply as energy gently flows into and out of you with every breath. All this energy aligns your energetic centers and reveals your truth to you. Start to breathe normally at a pace comfortable to you.

Breathe connective energy into your root chakra, a red-colored energy circling at the base of your spine. Feel grounded and safe. This energy genuinely helps you connect with your truth.

Breathe lively energy into your sacral chakra. There is orange colored energy circling at your pelvic floor and lower abdomen. Connect with your creativity and sexuality. This energy helps you to take pleasure in your truth.

Breathe engaging energy into your solar plexus—a yellow-colored energy circling the powerhouse in your belly. Realize your level of self-confidence and connection to your personal energy. This energy prepares you to act on your truth.

Breathe healing energy into your heart chakra. There's a green colored energy circling at the center of your chest. From here you can express love, compassion, and forgiveness. Through this energy you can learn to love your truth.

Breathe expressive energy into your throat chakra, a blue colored energy circling at the center of your neck. This energy center is for expressing, communicating, and listening. From this energy, learn to admire how you speak your truth.

Breathe insightful energy into your third eye, an indigo-colored energy circling between your eyebrows. This energy opens you up to your consciousness and inner wisdom. From this energy you can intuitively see your truth.

Breathe illuminating energy into your crown chakra. This is a violet-colored energy circling just above the top of your head. Through this energy you can experience divine enlightenment. From this energy, you can know your divine truth.

See a crystalline white energy circling your entire body, protecting you. Allow it to flow into your crown and flow through your body to your roots. Breathe in this safe, caring energy of the divine. You are connecting to your higher self, Source, and to Gaia. Take a few moments to just breathe. Be aware of your body, your energy, and your breath. It's okay if your mind wanders. Acknowledge what comes up. Let it be. It will float away as you return to your breath. You are in a safe place to just be.

All that you are, your entire being, is now full of healing energy, healing light of the divine. You are connected, alive, engaged, healed, expressive, insightful, and enlightened. You are authentic. Start to bring your attention back to your body. You are connected to the earth and the divine. Your personal magick ignited, and your vibration was high. Let the rays of your heart shine on all who pass by. When you are ready, open your eyes and return to this present experience.

Mix It Up

You can incorporate any type of healing energy work with your rituals or daily routines. For example, let's say your intention is to treat yourself better—find passion for life that makes you treat yourself as the important person that you are. Start off slow with a nightly routine that involves fire to ignite your inner spark and combine it with a self-care routine. Start off with an intention, such as, "I will treat myself better by putting my wellbeing first." Then say an affirmation, such as, "It is safe to love me for who I am." Then light a red candle (you can use white or pink if you don't have red). Take a ritual bath using herbs and oils that match your intention. Find different ways to incorporate crystals into your life. If you are busy, start doing this once a week on Tuesday. Gaze into the candle and start to visualize the life you want, a life where you matter, and a life where you are healthy enough to do the things you enjoy doing. To influence the intention of treating yourself better, take an engraved wooden comb and brush your hair or beard as you keep your gaze on the red candle. You can use any tool, healing modality, and energy discussed in this book together with lunar cycles to help you achieve your goals, deal with life's circumstances, or grow your spiritual practice.

9

LEARN ABOUT AND HEAL
YOUR ENERGY

What Is Energy Healing?

Everything is energy, including you. Subtle energy is an invisible force that drives your potential, affects your actions and reactions, and compels your intentions. Understanding energy helps you understand why and how life experiences happen, and the effect those experiences have on you. Air, or oxygen, is an accepted concept even though no one can see it, but some are hesitant to believe in energy because of its spiritual nature. Albert Einstein is best known for his equation $E = mc^2$, which states that energy and mass (matter) are the same thing, just in different forms.[32] Energy is vibration pulsing at myriad levels. A person's vibration (or the

---

[32] Michio Kaku, "Albert Einstein," https://www.britannica.com/biography/Albert-Einstein.

vibration of a place, thought, or thing) is an energetic quality. A vibration is a state expressed by mood, so a cheerful person's energy vibrates at a higher level than that of a person who is angry or sad. Your vibration affects your emotions and thought patterns, which can create beliefs that limit you in some capacity. Negative energy that affects your personal vibration can come in different forms, and these things cause energetic leaks that need healing.

Restoring your energetic body heals your physical and spiritual body, which creates energetic ripples that affect so much more than your personal world. As you heal yourself, you initiate generational healing, not only to your present family but also to generations into the future that you'll never have the opportunity to meet and to your ancestors. When you work with energy in this vast energetic network, including moon energy, it heals you by balancing weaknesses in your energetic field, thus raising your vibration. There are many types of energy to work with, such as lunar, earth, nature, seasons, spirit animal, directional, astrological, personal/inner spark, and the energy from your Source (God, universe, etc.). Remember, everything is connected.

How do you know if something you encounter on your spiritual journey is significant and linked to your current experience? The answer is simply how you interpret it; it is synchronic if the coincidence is meaningful to you. Synchronicities are perfectly timed incidents that cause us to momentarily consider divine possibilities. Our ancestors have observed repetitions of patterns and synchronicities for thousands of years. When you are connected, these make you curious and cause you to pay close attention, possibly even obsess a little. Curiosity may initiate a personal inquiry about your own true nature and what makes you authentic. You experience time-honored insights more and more as you begin to awaken spiritually.

As you develop your sixth sense, known as intuition, you may notice intrusive thoughts that make you feel uncomfortable or anxious. Living your truth is not easy, but in the long run it is much easier than living in La La Land. Reasoning based on hope (wishful thinking) is a fantasy or delusion that can make you feel comfortable, whereas reasoning based on fear is the loss of hope and killer of joy. Your intuition is a different beast altogether. You cannot reason with your inner knowing; it's a feeling—you just know. Reasoning comes from the thinking, egoic mind, whereas the connection your energy has to the energetic network is the source of your inner intuitive sense. Intuition is instinctual—you know or feel something before you have the facts or even meet a person. Strengthened inner knowing also creates more occurrences of synchronicity and makes you more magnetic, because energy runs in cycles and becomes intertwined. You develop your connection with all that is from your own spirit as you become open to receiving energetic messages and guidance that comes your way. Therefore, becoming more comfortable working with different types of energy creates more messages that increase the level at which your energy vibrates, thus further enhancing intuition.

The universe orchestrates moments of spiritual synchronicities, or winks from God, composed of perfectly aligned energy to deliver a divine message, provide guidance, or provide reassurance that you're on the right path. Divine messages add reason and purpose to your life as you move forward on your spiritual healing journey. If you are unsure of where to begin, ask for a sign and believe that all the powers that be will craft a special message just for you. The energetic network will ignite a spark in you through some energetic correlation if you give it permission to do so. The spark inside you generates an energetic flow that moves through your chakra system. As you work with energy, you will become more aware of how your thoughts control your reality. To begin, slow down and listen to your own inner voice. It doesn't matter if you believe in prayer, manifestation, magick, the placebo effect, or quantum physics; your thoughts can control your reality, and you can control your thoughts. Harness this power to begin your Wild Moon Healing journey.

Energetically Healing from Trauma

What is trauma? *Psychology Today* states that trauma is a person's response to a distressing experience.[33] The APA dictionary states it is any disturbing experience that results in a significant emotional response intense enough to have a long-lasting negative effect on a person's attitudes, behavior, and other aspects of functioning.[34] The Yahoo dictionary simply states that trauma is a deeply distressing or disturbing experience.[35] I've adopted the definition used by Elizabeth Power, M.Ed., of the Trauma Informed Academy. She defines trauma as "any event that so overwhelms a person, that they think they might die, lose their mind or be badly injured."[36] We have a vocabulary issue because people tend to use the word trauma loosely, and for many things. Some people confuse trauma with drama or use those words interchangeably, and, as such, words like disgusted, revolted, disappointed, or offended would be more appropriate to describe their situation, rather than trauma.

What truly matters is the effect or impact trauma has on you, rather than its name or definition, and how to control your emotions so you don't shift from calm to furious in a matter of seconds when triggered. Everyone has feelings, but we don't always manage them well. When the pain is too big to

---

[33] Psychology Today Staff, "Trauma," https://www.psychologytoday.com/us/basics/trauma.

[34] American Psychological Association, "Trauma," https://www.apa.org/topics/trauma/.

[35] Yahoo Dictionary, "Trauma," https://search.yahoo.com/search?fr=mcafee&type=E211US739G0&p=definition+of+trauma.

[36] "Trauma Informed Care." https://vickiegould.kartra.com/portal/jAUdZlyrvCrK/post/480.

tolerate, you push that pain down into your body. Physical pain in your body could be stored trauma, and energy work may help you self-regulate. You can learn to experience happiness as well as difficulty, and even feel fortunate in the midst of tough times. Learn to rely on the interconnections you have access to by connecting to this vast energetic network and learning to use this energy for its greatest good. Nothing discussed in this book replaces clinical work or a medical plan currently prescribed by your care providers. Tools such as talk therapy are great, but connecting to energy is more about a way of life and helping you to focus on the strengths you have that your life experiences (good and bad) helped develop. Collectively, people in the world need to stop focusing on lack, struggle, and the deficits their experiences may have caused.

All the things people do to themselves to survive could create a state of mental illness. I'm not talking about being resilient; I'm referring to how partaking in a behavior to reduce the effects of your current situation can turn into a lifelong struggle. For example, you might create protective boundaries, which, in turn, generates a state of loneliness. Or you might create the habit of having a drink to take the edge off, which spawns a lifelong struggle with alcoholism. Or, maybe eat to ease intense feelings, only to become morbidly obese. When you are just trying to make it through each day as it comes and someone labels you with a mental or health condition, or some sort of biological disorder, this adds more distress into your already stressful life. When you are fighting for some of the basics in life, such as safety and love, you're not learning the basics of self-care and how to love yourself. Recall, self-love makes the world go 'round, and it is sad that people have to learn how to do that rather than being taught how to love themselves properly during their upbringings. People who struggle to get through the day do not have a gene or chromosome mutation. What they may have is a hard life filled with struggle and lack of abundance.

My goal is to help people who do not like who they've become or the status of their life (i.e., the impact of their trauma) to energetically heal, transform their life, and become the person they were born to be. Ultimately, I want to help create a world where people don't have to learn to love themselves; rather, caregivers teach that from infancy, and it is a part of every child's cultural upbringing. For now, rather than exclusively talking about your past negative experiences, focus on how you've learned to transform to survive, even if surviving means you've adapted to please others, and recognize your strengths.

Being honest with yourself about the impact of your life experience(s) is a more gracious approach, rather than having a medical professional label you as having a mental illness. I do want to stress that I am not talking about a psychotic episode or something that does require medical attention. I'm talking about how everyday life weighs you down and how all your life experiences created the person you are today. Experiencing energetic leaks, such as undergoing trauma, struggle, and lack and people pleasing alter the very foundation of your soul and disrupt your connection to the vast energetic network available to you.

In my practice I don't tell you that I can heal your trauma because I can't. No one can heal trauma because it is an experience, and no one can change what has already occurred. However, you can alter the effects your trauma has on your mind and body through energy work, and what I do is support you, hold a safe place for you, and maybe help you resolve some of the impacts of an overwhelming experience. My personal journey is that of struggle and fighting for my own health as I was healing from so many other things. I am still working to heal my physical body from all the behaviors and habits born as a result of my trauma. We all do it… We all do something to help us get through or take the edge off. But then that thing becomes an addiction, and the addiction leads to physical issues in your body. Wild Moon Healing, or Moon work, is the approach I created to heal myself somatically and energetically, and now I'm sharing it with you.

Finding Your Energetic Theme

At this point in the book, you know the more you become aware of your energy and all that is around you and that you connect to, the more you can direct your life and the less outside forces affect the trajectory of your life. But, did you know that you have an energetic theme for your life that changes annually on your birthday? You can learn about your theme by studying profection years. Annual profections, a technique that is thousands of years old, is a component of Hellenistic Astrology.[37] It is one of the most efficient forecast techniques in astrology today that unlocks a unique perspective on your current life. The majority of the topics I've covered in this book have a cyclical nature, and this is no exception. It taps into the cyclical nature of time. With the annual profections, you move from one astrological house to the next each year on your birthday and stay in that house for one year (until your next birthday). The activated house is a window into the area of your life that will be highlighted for the following twelve months.

Each of the twelve houses connects to and rules different parts of your life and different energies. The year you are born, you are in a First House profection year. On your first birthday you move to the Second House profection year, and so on. Use the numbers on this wheel to find your age, or your current profection year. Whatever house your age appears in, this is a sense of the strong energy governing your life—it is the main energetic theme of your life right now.

---

[37] Blaze Maximus, "Introduction to Annual Profections," https://astrobymax.com/blog/annual-profections.

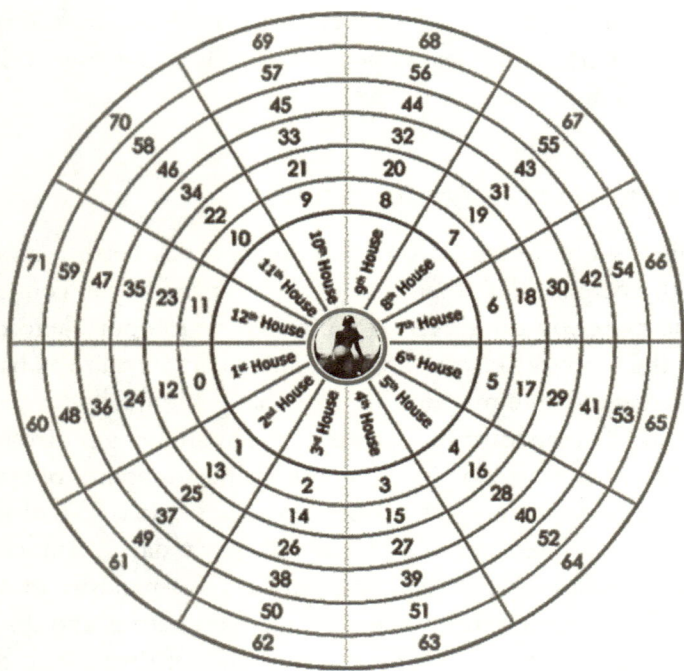

You can leave it right here for now, or you can look further into this energy using your birth chart.

Incorporating Your Birth Chart

Find your rising / ascendant sign on your birth chart. This is assigned in your First House profection year. From there each sign follows in order for each house. For example, let's say you're a Cancer Rising and you're 29 years old. Twenty-nine is a Sixth House profection year (as denoted from the above wheel). The Sixth House would be in Sagittarius. Recall your rising sign is assigned in your First House profection year, and each sign follows, so:

- Cancer = 1st House
- Leo = 2nd House
- Virgo = 3rd House

- Libra = 4th House
- Scorpio = 5th House
- Sagittarius = 6th House

This would mean Sagittarius plays a part in your Sixth House profection year. This would bring more Sagittarius energy to the mix—more opportunities, more optimism, and more expansion *(ruled by Sagittarius)*.

Energetic Influence per Zodiac

- Aries: more energy and drive, enthusiasm, excitement, impatience
- Taurus: stable and secure, grounded, confident, stubborn
- Gemini: ideas and plans, busy, variety, adaptable, scattered
- Cancer: emotions and comfort, support, nurturing, subjective
- Leo: creative and fun, romantic, friendly, attention, needy
- Virgo: work and chores, small projects, detailed, productive, anxious
- Libra: others and relationships, balance, peace, compromise, indecision
- Scorpio: transform and research, solutions, passion, intensity
- Sagittarius: expansion and exploration, travel, learning, optimism, arrogance
- Capricorn: goals and direction, practical, disciplined, responsibilities, traditional
- Aquarius: unconventional and different, change, charitable, aloof
- Pisces: intuitive and imaginative, compassionate, empathetic, sensitive

Planetary Influences

In using profection, there is a Time Lord, which is the natural ruling planet of the zodiac sign. This ruling planet sheds light on the quality of events and circumstances that take center stage during your profection year. Traditional rulers of each sign are (modern planets Uranus, Neptune, and Pluto aren't considered):

- Mars – Aries, Scorpio
- Venus – Taurus, Libra
- Mercury – Gemini, Virgo
- Moon – Cancer
- Sun – Leo
- Jupiter – Sagittarius, Pisces
- Saturn – Capricorn, Aquarius

In keeping with the above example of the Sixth House profection year in Sagittarius, the traditional ruler is Jupiter. Find Jupiter in your natal chart. The sign and house location of Jupiter, as well as the aspects it makes, will also factor into the energetic influence of the next year of your life. In your birth chart, if you have a house with no planets, that means you don't have to directly put a lot of effort into this aspect of your life, as the motion is guided by inertia (by other houses). In your natal chart, houses with planets are aspects of your life where you need to direct your energy, put in effort, learn lessons, and be active.

Numerology – Calculate Your Numbers

Numbers show your strengths and weaknesses, so understand them and how you can use the energy of your personal numbers to increase your vibrational flow. Your birth date is used to calculate your attitude number, life path, and birth number. The attitude number is related to the Sun and achievement. It describes how you present your energy to the world. Your life path number calculates who you are at your core. Your birth number is simply the day you were born and is reflective of the first impression you make on people. You can use the letters of your name to calculate your destiny number and soul's urge number. Your soul's urge number represents your inner self; it knows what you want, like, and dislike, what motivates you, and what you need. Your destiny number influences your personal strengths and also your challenges. Your power number speaks to your vocation and the energy available to you to build a career and accomplish goals in your life. Moreover, it's about how your contributions make a difference in the world and how you find satisfaction in life.

Calculations Based on Your Birthdate

Life Path Number

Your life path number is the most important number in your entire numerology chart. It is just as it sounds—a number that stands for the path you are on in this lifetime. It reveals the energy of your true soul (your identity, including strengths, weaknesses, talents, and ambitions) and the challenges you may be faced with in order to learn and grow into that person. Understanding the meaning of your life path number helps you see why things happen the way they do and gives you the power to move through any situation with purpose and intention. A life path number can be any single-digit number between 1 and 9. There are only three instances where a number is not reduced to a single digit. There are only three two-digit numbers called master numbers, and they are 11, 22, and 33. If you have a master number, then you have the ability to bring about big change in the world. Each number carries a different energy.

Your life path number shows your true nature, uniqueness as a person, and the karmic debt that you have to work through. You need your full birthday for this calculation. Someone born on August 12, 1990, would calculate their life path number as follows:

08 + 12 + 1990

Birth month: 0 + 8 = 8

Birthday: 1 + 2 = 3

Birth year: 1 + 9 + 9 + 0 = 19; then reduce 19 like 1 + 9 = 10; then reduce 10 like 1 + 0 = 1. Now you add all these numbers together (8 + 3 + 1 = 11). As eleven is a master number, you do not reduce it to a single-digit number. Life path number 11's are deeply intuitive and are meant to learn balance so they aren't overcome by their overwhelming empathy for others.

Life Path Titles

- Life Path One – The Leader, Inventor, or Creator
- Life Path Two – The Peacemaker
- Life Path Three – The Artist or Inspiration to Others
- Life Path Four – The Reliable Builder
- Life Path Five – The Adventurer or Learner
- Life Path Six – The Parent, Teacher, or Healer
- Life Path Seven – The Seeker, Philosopher, or Spiritual Teacher
- Life Path Eight – The Executive or Politician
- Life Path Nine – The Humanitarian or Philanthropist
- Life Path Eleven (Master Number 11) – The Empath
- Life Path Twenty-Two (Master Number 22) – Master Builder
- Life Path Thirty-Three (Master Number 33) – Enlightened Teacher

A side note to seeing multiple digits of the same number is that they are higher extensions of the basic one through nine.

Birth Number

The birthday number reveals how people see you at first glance; your first impression on the world. If your life path number is compatible with your birthday number, people can read you easily. But if your life path number is the total opposite of your birthday number, people will need more time to get to know you before they can really understand you. To calculate your birthday number, you simply use the day you were born. For example, if you were born on the 23rd, you would simply add 2 and 3 together for a birthday number of 5.

Birth Number Definitions

- Birth Number One (1, 10, 19, 28)
  You seem like someone who doesn't follow the status quo; someone who values their individuality above all else. You have a real leadership quality that others notice and follow. You command any room.
- Birth Number Two (2, 11, 20, 29)
  You seem trustworthy—someone who can see both sides of a situation and give fair advice and guidance. People are drawn to you because of your gentle nature and psychic abilities.
- Birth Number Three (3, 12, 21, 30)
  When people first meet you, you leave a big impression. You radiate joy and are quick to tell a funny story or crack a joke when you first meet someone. People often guess that you are an artist (or should be one) because they can feel your creative aura.

- Birth Number Four (4, 13, 22, 31)
  You seem serious—someone who can handle any situation in a quick, orderly manner. People are impressed by your ability to notice minute details and your no-nonsense way of speaking. You seem like a person who likes to get to the point.
- Birth Number Five (5, 14, 23)
  You seem like a bubbly extrovert. Your quick wit and fun-loving nature immediately charm those around you. You can easily strike up a conversation with anyone. People assume that you're always ready to party.
- Birth Number Six (6, 15, 24)
  When someone first meets you, they immediately feel your presence. You have a dynamic personality that people indulge in. Small children and animals especially seem to connect with you.
- Birth Number Seven (7, 16, 25)
  You are difficult to read. People don't quite know how to take you at first. It could be because they sense your intelligence and are intimidated by it, or because you are so quiet—they don't know what you're thinking. You have an air of mystery about you.
- Birth Number Eight (8, 17, 26)
  You like to be surrounded by quality. People assume you have excellent taste in clothes, food, and books and may ask you for recommendations. You also have a very intense nature that people notice and are intimidated by. Remember to show your warmth when meeting new people.
- Birth Number Nine (9, 18, 27)
  You come off as a helper, someone who can guide others through difficult problems and struggles. You have an air about you that makes people believe you have all the answers. You also seem friendly enough that they feel comfortable confiding in you with their troubles.

Attitude Number

Your attitude number is how you approach life and the energetic vibration you give off, as well as the vibrational imprint you leave behind. If you want to know how you handle life, then discover your attitude number. You simply add your birth month and the day of your birth together. So, someone born on March 23rd would calculate their attitude number like 3 + 2 + 3 = 11 = 1 + 1 = 2. There are no master numbers with this calculation, so add double digits together.

Attitude Number Definitions

- Attitude Number One
  You don't like to ask for help. You prefer to be self-sufficient and have control over your destiny. You are self-motivated: once you have a goal in mind, you will do whatever it takes to achieve it.
- Attitude Number Two
  You wear your heart on your sleeve. You have an easy-going nature and are willing to give people the benefit of the doubt. You are sensitive to the emotions of those around you. You're motivated by your desire to give and receive love.
- Attitude Number Three
  You are young at heart. Because of your natural enthusiasm and childlike wonderment, people often mistake you for being younger than you really are. Your moods are so big they can affect others—in both positive and negative ways. Luckily, your bad moods don't last long.
- Attitude Number Four
  You favor logic. You combat the chaos of life by making lists and keeping track of every detail. You are prepared for every situation that life can throw at you. Keeping organized is important to your well-being.

- Attitude Number Five
  You enjoy a carefree approach to life. For you, variety is the spice of life. You don't like routine and will often switch things up at a moment's notice. You view each day is a new adventure.
- Attitude Number Six
  You are a natural caregiver who instinctively nurtures others. You are the first to offer someone a place to stay or take a stray animal in. You take on responsibility with ease. You do well in high-stress situations where you spring into action and fix it.
- Attitude Number Seven
  You like to keep things close to the vest. You don't reveal your emotions easily but are constantly analyzing others. You are introspective and deeply spiritual, always searching to answer life's questions. You only reveal your thoughts and options to those you truly trust.
- Attitude Number Eight
  You have no problem telling people what you really think—and you don't sugar coat anything. You try to live honestly and have no use for phoniness. Your strong personality is driven by your ambition and work ethic. Money is important to you because it represents security and stability.
- Attitude Number Nine
  Your motto in life is, "How can I help others?" You are a humanitarian and compassionate leader. You want to make the world a better place. You'd be a great activist because of your social-consciousness and ability to attract loyal followers. Allow your generous heart to lead you through life.

Calculations Based on Your Name

Soul Urge Number

Your soul urge is also known as your heart's desire, and it represents what your heart and soul most crave in this world. When your heart desires something, it's expressed as dreams, hopes, or wishes. This calculation reveals your inner motivations and is a lens through which you make decisions. If this number is the same as your life path number, then you may find that being authentic comes easy to you. If they don't match, you may notice conflict, as if there is a tug of war between your head and your heart. See the "Numbers Strengths and Weaknesses" section for information about your number.

> To start your calculations, write out your full birth name on a single line.
> JANEJILLDOE
> Then identify the vowels listed in your name (i.e., remove the consonants).
> AEIOE

Assign each vowel its numerology number listed in The Key under the destiny number calculation in the next section. In some instances, the letter "Y" is counted as a vowel. Reduce your answer until you obtain a single digit.

$1 + 5 + 9 + 6 + 5 = 26 = 2 + 6 = 8$

The exceptions for reducing numbers are for the master numbers 11, 22, and 33. If your calculation yielded 10, you would reduce it to 1.

Soul Urge Number Summary

- Soul Urge Number One – Independent, self-sufficient, natural leader

- Soul Urge Number Two – Sensitive, emotional, intuitive
- Soul Urge Number Three – Engaging, congenial, natural entertainer
- Soul Urge Number Four – Stable, organized, disciplined
- Soul Urge Number Five – Charismatic, adventurous, explorer
- Soul Urge Number Six – Loyal, diplomatic, balanced
- Soul Urge Number Seven – Independent, analytical, educated
- Soul Urge Number Eight – Driven, ambitious, pursuit of material wealth
- Soul Urge Number Nine – Humanitarian, idealistic, broad perspective
- Soul Urge Number Eleven (Master Number) – You are on a unique spiritual journey in this lifetime. Well-developed and deep sense of morality. Intuitively connected to the collective.
- Soul Urge Number Twenty-Two (Master Number) – You are here to leave your mark on the world in some manner. You possess power and intuitive understanding. Your mark could be financial, spiritual, or even political.
- Soul Urge Number Thirty-Three (Master Number) – You have a pressing need to evolve spiritually— no matter how you define spirituality. If this is your soul number, you may struggle with a sense self-righteousness and control while infusing love and service in all that you do.

Destiny Number

Your destiny number reveals your heart's desires and what will create a feeling of fulfillment in your life, as well as challenges and opportunities you may encounter. This calculation is about what you are destined for and who you are destined to become. You calculate your destiny number using your first and last name and the key below to correspond the letters in your name to a number.

The Alphabet Key

- Use the number 1 for the letters A, J, S.
- Use the number 2 for the letters B, K, T.
- Use the number 3 for the letters C, L, U.
- Use the number 4 for the letters D, M, V.
- Use the number 5 for the letters E, N, W.
- Use the number 6 for the letters F, O, X.
- Use the number 7 for the letters G, P, Y.
- Use the number 8 for the letters H, Q, Z.
- Use the number 9 for the letters I, R.

Write out your full name across a piece of paper and list the corresponding number below it:

J A N E - J I L L - D O E

Jane is numerically expressed as: $1 + 1 + 5 + 5 = 12 = 1 + 2 = 3$

Jill is numerically expressed as: $1 + 9 + 3 + 3 = 16 = 1 + 7 = 8$

Doe is numerically expressed as: $4 + 6 + 5 = 15 = 1 + 5 = 6$

Then you add the numerical equivalent for your first, middle, and last names together ($3 + 8 + 6 = 17 = 1 + 7 = 8$). So, the destiny number is 8, deeming Jane is destined to make a difference in this world and will do so when she chooses to help others.

Destiny Number Definitions

- Destiny Number One

You are destined to be a leader that will rise to the top of your field. You live life to the fullest; however, you tend to burn the candle at both ends. "Work hard, play hard" is your motto; you are determined to achieve your full potential.

- Destiny Number Two
  You are destined to work for a cause and serve a higher purpose. You tend to struggle with codependency and neediness; learn to be strong on your own. Your fulfillment comes from achieving something powerful as part of the collective.

- Destiny Number Three
  You are destined to find your own niche in this world by living authentically and making a name for yourself. When you discover your truth and devote yourself fully to it, your creative center will explode with passion-driven intensity. If you find it difficult to understand your truth or find yourself unable to turn your passion and talents into something tangible, you may become self-destructive and depressed. One thing's for sure, your path will be unique.

- Destiny Number Four
  You are destined to create something lasting and valuable to the world (your legacy). It could be your actual family, created through biological, adopted, or fostered children, it could be a business, or it could relate to community impact. You may tend to be rigid and controlling, always striving for perfection.

- Destiny Number Five
  You are destined for great adventures that inspire others. They may say you march to the beat of your own drum, but you feel energy vibrating around you, which is more likely what you are marching to! You may have tendencies to be self-centered or demanding. Once you

define your own boundaries and can live life without spiraling, you will live life fully and well.

- Destiny Number Six
Your destiny derives from your natural ability to nurture. You love to be of service to others, create harmony in every situation, heal people and relationships, and give your time and energy to the weak who have no voice. Make sure to steer away from helping others resolve their problems—they may blame you for the outcome, and you may come out feeling resentful or used.

- Destiny Number Seven
You are destined to teach, guide, or counsel because you are all about knowledge—and what is knowledge if not shared? Your need for solitude could lead to getting lost in your own head, while your thirst for knowledge could cause you to become a cynic. Being optimistic and finding hope is important to your mental health.

- Destiny Number Eight
Once your inner spark is ignited, you are destined to make a difference in the world. You will learn that making material success can only provide so much happiness or reward. When you choose to use your success to help others, you have the potential to create a life-changing legacy. The struggle in your life comes from resisting greed, corruption, and selfishness at all costs. If you fail at this life lesson, you may be lost in immorality forever.

- Destiny Number Nine
You are destined to become your best self through a journey of discovery. The pursuit of knowledge will never end for you, so you never become dogmatic about what you already know—there's always more to learn! Your path is difficult regarding the aspect of

learning to love yourself completely and appreciating others without trying to change them. You actually do not know best… for everyone.

- Destiny Master Number Eleven
  This number is made up of double ones, and also the sum of two. This destiny path is the cumulation of leadership and healing. You may struggle with being in the limelight versus the shadows throughout your entire life. Strong feelings of imposter syndrome may keep you from leading and healing others. Overcoming this inner turmoil is a major part of your story. Your unique gifts are intended to be shared and will benefit the collective.
- Destiny Master Number Twenty-two
  This number is made up of double twos, and also the sum of four. As a master number, you have a humanitarian mission in life, so your destiny is to build projects that will benefit everyone. You may wrestle with the exposure your corporate talents bring to your personal life—part of you yearns for a quieter life.
- Destiny Master Number Thirty-Three
  This number is made up of double threes, and also the sum of six. As a master number thirty-three, you are destined to save the world through love and unity—no pressure! You are truly here to make a difference. Focus on bringing people together rather than picking a side. Your struggles come from your own making—you placed the burden on your shoulders. This is your path, but you will lead and inspire, all for the greater good.

Power Number

Your power number is simply obtained by adding your destiny number and your life path number, then reducing to a single digit. The energy this number describes can lay dormant in you until your mid-forties. The power or aggressiveness of this influence this number will have when activated depends on if the number is identical to one of your other core numbers calculated above. If the number is identical to one of your core numbers, then your current energy is enhanced, and if it is different, a new energetic theme may be introduced in your life—this is one of the places mid-life crises come from (remember also being stuck in the spiritual nature of number two).

The definition of your power number is the same as listed under the life path number. When this energy of this number takes over, it stays to influence the rest of your life.

Body Pendulum

Have a simple yes/no question about something but don't want to pull your pendulum for fear of ridicule? Then use your body as a pendulum to conduct what is called a sway test. This is a form of muscle testing providing you with a tool to bypass your conscious mind to obtain biofeedback directly from your subconscious. While standing tall and still, settle into a calm, quiet mindset as best you can within your current environment. Now ask a question. Posing the question in your mind is okay. You don't have to articulate it because you are speaking with your higher self to access your deep inner wisdom, without your "thinking brain" getting in the way. Possibly even before you begin to ask the question, your body may start to sway.

The sway can be different for everyone, just as with a yes/ no responses from a pendulum. Options could be, if your body sways forward the answer is yes, and if your body sways backwards, the answer is no. Alternatively, if your body sways forwards and backwards, the answer is yes, while a side-to-side sway (or left and right) indicates an answer of no.

Journaling

Look at journaling as a pendulum of sorts because only you have the answers you seek, and journaling can access your higher self. Many times, I'm writing and I think, "Where did all this even come from?" or I go in a completely different direction from where I started. Whatever you are trying to figure out or change in your life, you already have the answers and know what to do. Conflict only arises because you don't want to do what you know you should do or what is in your best interest. Maybe you have divergent ideas that conflict with your principles, complicated relationships, or issues with a family member. Maybe you need to unravel your principles in order to unlearn them and learn your truth. Anything that is complicated in your life is your own doing. The only way to uncomplicate something is to do that thing that you know you should do but is hard to do or you just don't want to do. Internal conflict doesn't exist when you are living in alignment with your truth (i.e., living authentically).

Nothing outside of yourself can help you create change in your life, so write about it. The answers you seek are inside you, and writing can help get all that information out of you so you can better understand the complexities of it all. You can ask yourself exploratory questions or follow pre-determined prompts. By putting pen to paper, you engage with a special energy that you cannot achieve with visualizations alone, or even by typing on an electronic device. By writing you are thinking and doing at the same time. It's the way your body and mind work together in the process to lead you to find richer content inside. Journaling is intimate and an important activity to discover and understand your thoughts and feelings.

Journaling about what vocation you want in life while harnessing the energy of the moon and perhaps the energy of Artemis, Greek goddess of the hunt, can help you pursue and reach your career goals. Journaling can help you find answers to your spending habits, but doing so under a Taurus lunar influence while working with the energy of a squirrel spirit animal who hoards nuts can help you reduce spending and increase your savings. Just as working with crystals can amplify your energy, journaling has the same effect, only through journaling you are raising your own energetic vibration.

A little trick when journaling to access your inner child: write with your non-dominant hand. This is harder to do and requires more focus and attention (i.e., it engages mindfulness). Technically, doing this gives you greater access to the right-brain functions and feminine energy to include feelings, intuition, gut instinct, inner wisdom, and spirituality. Start writing with your non-dominant hand and answer questions like the following as you go. Don't think about the questions, just read them and write. Did you attempt to fix mistakes in spelling or grammar as you wrote? Did you judge yourself for poor penmanship? Did you go as slow as you could to be as neat as possible? These are all clues to what is driving your behavior (as directed by your inner child). When you're done, go back and read what your inner critic had to say about you.

Journaling is powerful. Your thinking mind complicates simple things by judging, overthinking, procrastinating, and failing to plan. You also complicate your life when you are unwilling to go on an inner journey because of fear, anger, resentment, or a host of other negative feelings that dominate your mind. So, by adding meditation to your routine, you can create a still and peaceful environment from which to begin. Human beings are complex in nature, and our emotions are multifaceted. Connecting with or invoking different energies to help you magnifies the process and your personal growth.

Zodiac Decan

I feel the need to touch on this topic, as Wild Moon Healing is about discovering your truth and living an authentic life.

Each zodiac sign has qualities that you can use to characterize a person born under that sign. In astrology, I've heard a Gemini can be two-faced, a Taurus is more stubborn than a bull, and a Virgo is so nit-picky that their behavior will drive you mad! Have any of these generalizations left you feeling alone and misunderstood because you don't relate? The reason is each sign of the zodiac has three different versions of itself.

The ancient Babylonians created the zodiac wheel by dividing the sky into four equal sections designated by the yearly equinoxes and solstices.[38] Each of these four sections of sky were further divided into three sections measuring 30 degrees each. This gives us a full 360-degree zodiac circle with twelve equal sections of 30 degrees each. Think back to sacred geometry; the power of nine is a 360-degree circle—it's in everything. The individual zodiac signs are the 30-degree sections of space that were mathematically calculated in a way that was, and still is, intimately connected to our yearly seasons. To get to know yourself better let's explore the three different versions of each sign known as a "decan" and made up of 10 degrees. The first decan is 0 – 10 degrees, the second stretches over 11 – 20 degrees, and the third encompasses 21 – 30 degrees. Each sign accounts for 28 days, but since there are only twelve signs and the moon takes approximately 29.5 days to transit the Earth, these decans will be approximations of dates on the calendar depending on the shifting degrees.

Finding a secondary ruler for your sign, or which decan you are in, is based on something called "triplicity." This refers to a group of zodiac signs represented by the same element. Here are the common assignments of the elements to the triplicities:

- Fire: Aries, Leo, Sagittarius
- Earth: Taurus, Virgo, Capricorn

[38] Corinne Lane, "A Short History of Astrology," https://astrolibrary.org/short-history-of-astrology/.

- Air: Gemini, Libra, Aquarius
- Water: Cancer, Scorpio, Pisces

Researching a sign's sub-ruler can provide you with a deeper understanding of who you are and what makes you tick. So, if you have the Sun sign of Aries, and were born on the 15th of the month, you may exhibit more traits of the second decan, Leo. For myself, I was left thinking, "This still doesn't totally represent me" after researching my signs decans. For this reason, make sure you research your birth chart or speak to an astrologer to gain an even better understanding of yourself.

10

CONCLUSION

Final Thoughts

I hope that the knowledge you gained about yourself while reading this book helps to spark a personal revolution in you. Human beings are designed to create and achieve incredible things. It is through your personal gifts and authenticity that you can bring your personal revolution to the world. The reason so many people do not reach this level of achievement and fulfillment is because we experience trauma, have negative life experiences, remain stuck in a story, forget who we are, or were never taught how to be authentic and love ourselves. There is a desire deep within you. All that you want, your hopes, dreams, and aspirations, are yours for a reason—they will help lead you to your purpose.

Use the information in this book to learn more about yourself. Get to know you and learn to love you. When you do this, you can overcome mistakes, find courage, and face your fears. Everything starts with you—one person can make a difference. You don't have to make a grand gesture; subtle action can lead to a revolution. By refusing to give up her seat on a bus, Rosa Parks propelled the anti-segregation movement. Brave resistance from the passengers of Flight 93 prevented even more tragedy from occurring on one of the darkest days of U.S. history. J.K. Rowling, author of the Harry Potter series, inspired a new generation of readers. Not one of these people woke up and said, "I'm going to change the world today." However, they lived authentically, did what was right (and courageous), and followed their hearts.

Whatever revolution you are here to start may not be easy, but then, when you come from a place of authenticity and self-love, it may come naturally. As this book concludes, I leave you with some final important thoughts...

- Make energy your first language—understand more than words spoken in any language. If it's your calling, it will keep energetically showing up until you listen. You might as well follow your truth and live authentically because your vibe will tell everyone the truth anyway.

- Engage with the energetic network and use all the different types of energy by engaging in Wild Moon Healing and following lunar cycles to create your best life. The necessary components to Moon work and connecting with different types of energy are awareness, intention, being present, and purpose.

- The most important concept about the energetic network to understand is that energy is honest. You can be a master of hiding your feelings or self-deceit, but your energy does not lie.

- Your Source bears no ill or harm to you. When working with energy, you will receive only one of three responses from the energy that is above: "Yes,"

"Not right now," and "I have something better in store for you."

- The inner reality creates the outer form; your subconscious mind controls the vibration of your energy and the reality of your life. What you accept, whether fact or fiction (the subconscious cannot differentiate) affects your vibrational frequency. Regardless of the validity of your thinking (maybe it's a false and limiting belief), when you accept something, you become emotionally involved, and it is real.

- The geography of your emotions (i.e., living in a place of grief, uncertainty, or love) will positively or negatively affect the inspired action you take during each lunar cycle. Use energy to change where you are. You have the ability to change the vibration of your energy at any moment in time.

- Your physical being is connected to spiritual energy. Your anatomy includes an aura, meridians, and chakra energy centers that are affected by your daily choices in similar ways as your physical body. The dis-ease in your body may be from a spiritual need or energetic deficiency.

- Energetic signs come in many forms, such as feathers, coins, birds, butterflies, numbers, animals, flickering lights, or rainbows. Even memories, music, or fragrances come to you for a purpose. Pay attention. They mean something.

- When you create a practice of following lunar cycles to create your best life, you will notice how energy affects you and eventually you will learn how to use it to find balance.

- Intention is key to everything. Create an intention under a new moon or get lost in some Pisces energy (dreaming and wanting). This is a form of energetic devotion to your spiritual beliefs. How downtrodden are those with no aspirations? Dream big.

- Inspired action under a waxing moon helps you to escape the trap that exists within the world of your thoughts because you may be stuck in a place of self-deceit or false beliefs. You were created to experience the true reality of life, so get out there and do things!
- Shadow work under a full moon is about gaining critical awareness of self, beliefs, and situations. Look for signs or synchronicities that may provide encouragement or guidance along your journey.
- Develop a practice under a waning lunar phase that teaches you to always show yourself grace and respect—give yourself permission to forgive yourself for anything in your past that haunts you. Tap into the energy of divine spiritual guides, specific deities, or energy from animals or nature to help you increase your vibration.
- Don't ever give up on yourself or your journey. Keep the faith and be patient. You are worth your effort!

Travel authentically.

CONTINUED
HEALING SUPPORT

To continue with your healing and spiritual journey, manifest your goals and dreams, and achieve your best life in a supportive and safe environment, sign up for my FREE members' content page on my website, wildmoonhealers.com. There, you will have access to content, such as a new moon intention worksheet and an intention contract form. You can also learn about my personalized and group life-coaching services.

On my website, you can also:

- Sign up to receive newsletters containing encouraging and action-oriented information.
- Follow my blog to receive an email every time I post a new blog.
- Follow Wild Moon Healers on social media: Facebook, Pinterest, Instagram, and Twitter.
- Listen to my blogs and other content on my podcast.

- Purchase Book 1 and the Wild Moon Healing oracle deck to support your moon work.

I sincerely appreciate you and the time you have spent reading *Wild Moon Healing Revolution*. May I ask you for a favor? I would love it if you could leave your honest review on the retail site of your preference. And, because I wrote this book in service to all who read it, I would love to know your opinion on how I can improve my message or how my message has supported positive change in your life. Please visit my website and leave your comments there. Thank you!

After reading my book, I hope you desire to become a Wild Moon Healer—and become your best self!

I look forward to interacting with you online.

Authentically me,
Donna S. Conley

APPENDIX ONE

Table of Zodiac Elements, Qualities, and Polarities

Sign	Element	Quality	Polarity
Aries	Fire	Cardinal	Yang (+)
Taurus	Earth	Fixed	Yin (-)
Gemini	Air	Mutable	Yang (+)
Cancer	Water	Cardinal	Yin (-)
Leo	Fire	Fixed	Yang (+)
Virgo	Earth	Mutable	Yin (-)
Libra	Air	Cardinal	Yang (+)
Scorpio	Water	Fixed	Yin (-)
Sagittarius	Fire	Mutable	Yang (+)
Capricorn	Earth	Cardinal	Yin (-)
Aquarius	Air	Fixed	Yang (+)
Pisces	Water	Mutable	Yin (-)

APPENDIX TWO

Energetic Sigil

My extraordinarily talented sister, Lara, was gifted with the skill of art. She does energetic sketches (sigils) as they come to her. One day, out of the blue, she heard a message that was intended for me, "Healing is my birthright." So, she started drawing, and this is her finished sigil.

The willow tree has a long history of healing. The willow manufactures an actual medicinal compound for relieving pain and is used in remedies such as aspirin. The "weeping" willow is known for its downward-facing branches, appearing as if it's grieving and crying. The willow has a gentle nature that reminds us to go inward just as the moon does and reminds us that it's okay to cry. Its spiritual nature relates to feminine energy and watery things such as emotions, vision, intuition, and divination. The words, "Healing Is My Birthright," and the willow tree on the sigil is a reflection of me as a healer. I am the tree, and the tree is me. It represents everything I need and all that I am.

Thank you, Lara, for sharing your incredible talent with me. I absolutely love it! Keep sharing your art with the world!

APPENDIX THREE

Zodiac Quick Reference

Here are some keywords associated with each sign to help you get started on your lunar journey. If any of these words feel like an energy that you need more of in your life, then work with the energy of that sign, house, and planet. If you resonate with any of the negative adjectives, work with the opposite sign (polarity) to help balance your energy.

- **Aries:** The first sign in the zodiac, associated with vigor and new beginnings, with a motto of "I am." Plant seeds of intention (or goals) under this new moon. *Positive Words* – Identity, self, individuality, fire, beginnings, adventurous, energetic, courageous, pioneering, enthusiastic, dynamic, and quick-witted. *Negative Words* – Selfish, quick-tempered, impulsive, impatient, boastful, and intolerant.
- **Taurus:** The second zodiac sign, associated with material pleasure, with a motto of "I have." Sow seeds of connection under this new moon. *Positive*

Words – Mother Earth, art, nature, body positivity, grounding, patient, reliable, warm-hearted, loving, persistent, determined, affectionate, sensuous, and easy-going. *Negative Words* – Jealous, possessive, resentful, inflexible, self-indulgent, greedy, laziness, and inflexibility.

- **Gemini:** The third sign of the zodiac, associated with youth and versatility, with a motto of "I think." Plant the seeds of your dreams under this new moon. *Positive Words* – Communicative, air, information, knowledge, social, adaptable, versatile, witty, intellectual, eloquent, youthful, and lively. *Negative Words* – Nervous, tense, superficial, inconsistent, cunning, nosy, intrusive, and interfering.

- **Cancer:** The fourth sign of the zodiac, associated with family and domesticity, with a motto of "I feel." Sow seeds of intention on your secrets under this new moon. *Positive Words* – Water, womb, mother, moon, comfort, emotional, loving, intuitive, imaginative, shrewd, cautious, protective, and sympathetic. *Negative Words* – Changeable, moody, overemotional, touchy, clinging, or unable to let go.

- **Leo:** The fifth sign of the zodiac, associated with making an impression, with a motto of "I will." Sow seeds of confidence under this new moon. *Positive Words* – Fire, creativity, fame, Sun, sovereignty, determined, assertive, driven, regal, dignified, magnanimous, generous, hospitable, caring, warm, authoritative, warmhearted, creative, enthusiastic, broad-minded, faithful, loyal, and loving. *Negative Words* – Pompous, patronizing, bossy, interfering, dogmatic, and intolerant.

- **Virgo:** The sixth sign of the zodiac, associated with purity and service, with a motto of "I analyze." No planting seeds; decide where to go from here. *Positive*

Words – Earth, goddess, harvest, sorting out what's necessary from what's not, modest, shy, meticulous, reliable, practical, diligent, intelligent, and analytical. *Negative Words* – Fussy, worry, anxiety, overcritical, harsh, perfectionist, or too conservative.

- **Libra:** The seventh sign of the zodiac, associated with justice, with a motto of "I balance." Plant seeds of balance under this new moon. *Positive Words* – Balance, justice, beauty, harmony, air, ideas, diplomatic, urbane, romantic, charming, easygoing, sociable, idealistic, and peace-loving. *Negative Words* – Indecisive, changeable, gullible, easily influenced, flirtatious, and self-indulgent.

- **Scorpio:** The eighth sign of the zodiac, associated with intensity, passion, and power, with a motto of "I lust." Sow seeds of expansion and transformation under this new moon. *Positive Words* – Deep waters, underworld, shadow, the past, determined, emotional, intuitive, powerful, passionate, exciting, and magnetic. *Negative Words* – Jealous, resentful, compulsive, obsessive, secretive, or obstinate.

- **Sagittarius:** The ninth sign of the zodiac, associated with travel and expansion, with a motto of "I see." Sow seeds of optimism under this new moon. *Positive Words* – Adventure, fire, the unknown, wildness, optimistic, freedom-loving, jovial, good-humored, honest, straightforward, intellectual, and philosophical. *Negative Words* – Blindly optimistic, careless, irresponsible, superficial, tactless, and restless.

- **Capricorn:** The tenth sign of the zodiac, associated with hard work and business affairs, with a motto of "I use." Sow seeds of resilience under this new moon. *Positive Words* – Earth, structure, integrity, hard work, practical, prudent, ambitious, disciplined, patient, responsible, stable, trustworthy, careful, humorous, and reserved. *Negative Words* – Pessimistic, derisory, grudging, coldness, conservatism, rigidity, materialism, and dullness.

- **Aquarius:** The eleventh sign of the zodiac, associated with future ideas and the unusual, with a motto of "I know." Plant seeds of innovation under this new moon. *Positive Words* – Air, new ideas, revolution, future-oriented, outsiders, Friendly, humanitarian, honest, loyal, original, inventive, independent, and intellectual. *Negative Words* – Intractable, contrary, perverse, unpredictable, unemotional, and detached.

- **Pisces:** The twelfth and last sign of the Zodiac, associated with human emotions, with a motto of "I believe." Sow seeds of hope under this new moon. *Positive Words* – Ocean, collective consciousness, mystical, dreams, imaginative, sensitive, compassionate, kind, selfless, unworldly, and intuitive. Sympathetic. *Negative Words* – Escapist, idealistic, secretive, vague, weak-willed, and easily manipulated.

BIBLIOGRAPHY

Books

Trismegistus, Hermes. *The Emerald Tablet of Hermes*. Digitized by Watchmaker Publishing. (Merchant Books, 2013).

Electronic

Albuquerque, Carlos. "The Twelve Olympians in the Zodiac." Medium. Accessed 23 Jun 2022, https://mullerornis. medium.com/the-twelve-olympians-in-the-zodiac-30379 0337412#:~:text=Aries%20is%20associated%20with%20 the%20head%2C%20and%20anyone,all%20traits%20 intrinsic%20to%20Athena%20in%20her%20myths.

Alphabet.net. "Goddess ISIS: Symbol, Meaning, Facts and Images." Accessed June 23, 2023, https://www.alphapedia. net/goddess-isis/.

American Psychological Association. "Trauma." Accessed July 31, 2023, https://www.apa.org/topics/trauma/.

Anderson, Micheline. "The Spiritual Heart, A Scientific Inquiry." The HeartMath Institute. Accessed June 30, 2023, https://www.heartmath.org/articles-of-the-heart/spiritual-heart/.

Aple, Thomas. "Roman Goddess Juno." Mythopedia. Accessed June 23, 2023, https://mythopedia.com/topics/juno.

Astrology Library. "12 Astrological Houses – Astrology Lesson 4." Accessed June 24, 2023, https://astrolibrary.org/.

Brahier, John. "Beauty, Bees, and God: The Fibonacci Sequence as a Theological Springboard in Secondary Mathematics." Accessed July 31, 2023, chrome-extension://efaidnbmnnnibpcajpcglclefindmkaj/https://files.eric.ed.gov/fulltext/EJ1231335.pdf.

Cambridge University Press. "Meaning of Ritual in English." Accessed July 31, 2023, https://dictionary.cambridge.org/us/dictionary/english/ritual.

Doniger, Wendy. "Kali." Encyclopedia Britannica. April 27, 2023, https://www.britannica.com/topic/Kali.

Esbats, Diana. "Goddess Diana." Coven of the Goddess. January 11, 2020, https://www.covenofthegoddess.com/goddess-diana/.

Fraga, Kaleena. "Inside Nikola Tesla's 3, 6, 9 Obsession And The Unusual Theories It Spawned." August 16, 2021, https://allthatsinteresting.com/nikola-tesla-3-6-9.

Greenberg, Mike. "Fortuna: Goddess of Luck in Rome." Mythologysource.com. February 22, 2021, https://mythologysource.com/fortuna-goddess-of-luck/.

Kaku, Michio. "Albert Einstein – A German American Physicist." *Encyclopedia Britannica*. June 8, 2023, https://www.britannica.com/biography/Albert-Einstein.

Kight, Jane. "What Is Sacred Geometry? The Ultimate Beginner's Guide." Omina. August 16, 2021, https://www.omniaradiationbalancer.com/blogs/news/sacred-geometry-beginners-guide.

Lane, Corinne. "A Short History of Astrology." Astrology Library. October 18, 2018, https://astrolibrary.org/short-history-of-astrology/.

Macquire, Kelly. "Hathor the Egyptian Goddess of Love, Beauty and Pleasure." *World History Encyclopedia*. June 5, 2022, https://www.worldhistory.org/video/2781/hathor-the-egyptian-goddess-of-love-beauty-and-ple/.

Maximus, Blaze. "Introduction to Annual Profections." Astrobymax.com. November 6, 2021, https://astrobymax.com/blog/annual-profections.

NASA. "Earth's Moon – Our Natural Satellite." NASA Solar System Exploration. July 27, 2022, https://solarsystem.nasa.gov/moons/earths-moon/in-depth/.

Numerologist.com. "So What's The Meaning of the Number 9?!" Accessed July 5, 2023, https://numerologist.com/numerology/meaning-of-the-number-9/.

Psychology Today Staff. "Trauma." *Psychology Today*, Accessed July 31, 2023, https://www.psychologytoday.com/us/basics/trauma.

Pursey, Kristie. "6 Nicola Tesla Quotes That Might Change The Way You See the World." April 17, 2017, https://www.learning-mind.com/nikola-tesla-quotes/#google_vignette.

Regula, de Traci. "Gaia: The Greek Goddess of the Earth." Thought Co., June 26, 2019, https://www.thoughtco.com/greek-mythology-gaia-1525978.

Rhys, Dani. "Apollo and Artemis – Greek Mythology." Symbolsage. January 26, 2021, https://symbolsage.com/apollo-and-artemis-mythology/.

Robertson, Katie. "What's 'IC' in the Birth Chart?" Astrology.com. January 24, 2023, https://www.astrology.com/article/ic-astrology/.

Shah, Parita. "What the Chakras Teach Us About the Mind and Body Connection." Chopra. April 2, 2020, https://chopra.com/articles/what-the-chakras-teach-us-about-the-mind-and-body-connection.

Shuttleworth, Martyn. "Mesopotamian Astronomy." Explorable. com. October 10, 2010, https://explorable.com/meso potamian-astronomy.

Stewart, Ian. "Number Symbolism." *Encyclopedia Britannica*. November 4, 2020, https://www.britannica.com/topic/ number-symbolism.

Tannous, Alexandre. "About Alexandre Tannous." Sound Meditation.com. Accessed June 24, 2023, https://sound meditation.com/about/.

Temple Purohit. "Goddess Saraswati – Hindu Goddesses and Deities." Accessed June 23, 2023, https://www.temple purohit.com/hindu-goddesses-and-deities/goddess-saraswati-hindu-goddesses-and-deities/.

Temple Purohit. "Goddess Lakshmi – Hindu Goddesses and Deities." Accessed June 23, 2023, https://www.templepurohit. com/hindu-goddesses-and-deities/goddess-lakshmi-hindu-goddesses-and-deities/.

"Trauma Informed Care." Life Changing Energy. Accessed June 20, 2023. Video, 0:06:09, https://vickiegould.kartra. com/portal/jAUdZlyrvCrK/post/480.

Thesleff, Holger. "Pythagoreanism." *Encyclopedia Britannica*. May 15, 2020, https://www.britannica.com/science/ Pythagoreanism.

Turnbull, Liz. "Kuan Yin: Goddess of Compassion" Goddess Gift. October 31, 2022, https://goddessgift.com/goddesses/ kuan-yin/.

Walker, Ned. "The Spiritual Significance of the Number 6." Bahai Teachings. Accessed June 30, 2023, https:// bahaiteachings.org/spiritual-significance-number-6/.

Williams, Susan. "What Is Gyan Mudra? 10 Benefits of the Yogic Hand Gesture for Peace." Yoga Practice. October 2023. https://yogapractice.com/yoga/gyan-mudra/.

Yahoo Dictionary. "Trauma." Access July 31, 2023, https:// search.yahoo.com/search?fr=mcafee&type=E211US 739G0&p=definition+of+trauma.

ABOUT THE AUTHOR

Determined to become an advocate for mental health, Donna S. Conley developed an integrated approach to teach people to discover who they are, what they want, and how to love and accept themselves so they can live their best lives. She began a career as a life coach, blogger, podcaster, and wrote the bestselling book *Wild Moon Healing* while working full-time in corporate America. Donna is working toward her goal of transitioning to a full-time career to help remove the stigma of mental health and normalize loving, committing to, believing in, and respecting yourself.

Donna has had a successful career in the human resources field for over twenty years. She earned a master's degree in her field from UMUC. Human resources is the business of people, and Donna has professionally helped, supported, and touched the lives of many people during her career. She is a trauma-informed energy coach who earned a coaching certification through Duke's DHWCT program and is a Reiki practitioner. She is also certified in sound healing, breathwork, and is a certified meditation teacher. Donna embodies these healing modalities in her coaching. She is currently enrolled at the Elementum Coaching Institute to further her somatic training and fully embody the skills necessary to bring her best self into her coaching programs to help others.

She was born and raised in Riva, Maryland, but has always considered Reedy, West Virginia, her home. That is where her mind wanders when she thinks about growing up and the summers she spent at her Nan Nan's. Donna is the proud mother of a United States Marine. If you can't find her, she's most likely in the woods discovering a new trail to hike or simply admiring the moon.

From a total wellness perspective and addressing people as a whole, she believes strongly in the spiritual aspects of health in addition to physical and mental health. She deeply believes everyone has their own inner magic and can use it to create their best life and inspire others.

INDEX